The Shape of the City
Toronto Struggles with Modern Planning

Critics have long voiced concerns about the wisdom of living in cities and the effects of city life on physical and mental health. For a century, planners have tried to meet these issues. John Sewell traces changes in urban planning, from the pre-Depression garden cities to postwar modernism and a revival of interest in the streetscape grid.

In this far-ranging review, Sewell recounts the arrival of modern city planning with its emphasis on lower densities, limited-access streets, segregated uses, and considerable green space. He makes Toronto a case history, with its pioneering suburban development in Don Mills and its other planned communities, including Regent Park, St Jamestown, Thorncrest Village, and Bramalea.

The heyday of the modern planning movement was in the 1940s to the 1960s, and the Don Mills concept was repeated in spirit and in style across Canada. Eventually, strong public reaction brought modern planning almost to a halt within the City of Toronto. The battles centred on saving the Old City Hall and stopping the Spadina Expressway. Sewell concludes that although the modernist approach remains ascendant in the suburbs, the City of Toronto has begun to replace it with alternatives that work.

This is a reflective but vigorous statement by a committed urban reformer. Few Canadians are better suited to point the way towards city planning for the future.

JOHN SEWELL was Chair of the 1991–3 Commission on Planning and Development Reform in Ontario. After working as a community organizer in Toronto neighbourhoods, he was first elected to Toronto City Council in 1969 and served as mayor from 1978 to 1980. Author of *Up Against City Hall* (1972) and *Police: Urban Police in Canada* (1986), he has also been urban affairs columnist for the *Globe and Mail* and chair of the Metro Toronto (Public) Housing Authority (1986–8).

Praise for *The Shape of the City*

'This city owes John Sewell yet another debt. The one-time community activist, one-time city councillor and one-time mayor has rewarded Torontophiles with a new book: *The Shape of the City*'
Colin Vaughan, *The Globe & Mail*

'Sewell not only understands the issues, he spells them out with clarity and passion. And though highly critical, he is no mere agent of historical scorn. He offers detailed perspective on what must be done if the dysfunctional results of postwar planning – suburbs, mega-buildings, transit and road systems – are to be invigorated and humanized.'
Charles Wilkins, *Canadian Geographic*

'The book's argument, clear and frequently dramatic, is only part of its pleasures. *The Shape of the City* can also be considered as a sort of Rosetta stone for the physical language of Toronto, an interpretive guide to the abstract map of the city's development, both visible and invisible.'
John Ferguson, *The Toronto Star*

Winner of The Toronto Historical Board 1994 Award of Merit

JOHN SEWELL

THE SHAPE OF THE CITY
Toronto Struggles with Modern Planning

UNIVERSITY OF TORONTO PRESS

Toronto Buffalo London

© University of Toronto Press Incorporated 1993
Toronto Buffalo London
Printed in Canada
Paperback reprinted 1993, 1995, 2002, 2007, 2010
ISBN 978-0-8020-2901-0 (cloth)
ISBN 978-0-8020-7409-6 (paper)

∞

Printed on acid-free paper

Canadian Cataloguing in Publication Data

Sewell, John, 1940–
The shape of the city:
Toronto struggles with modern planning

Includes bibliographical references and index.
ISBN 0-8020-2901-9 (bound) ISBN 0-8020-7409-x (pbk.)

1. City planning – Ontario – Toronto. I. Title.
HT169.C32T67 1993   352.9'6'09713541   C93-093598-5

For permission to reprint, the author and publisher
are grateful to Margaret Atwood for excerpts from
The Journals of Susanna Moodie, and to Dennis Lee for
the poem, 'The Day They Stopped the Spadina.'

Every attempt has been made to identify and credit
sources for illustrations. The publisher would appreciate
receiving information as to any inaccuracies in the credits
for subsequent editions.

Publication of this book has been assisted
by a grant from Hollinger Inc.
Assistance also came from the Canada Council
and the Ontario Arts Council
under their block grant programs.

To my parents,

for their constant support and encouragement

Contents

Foreword

Once upon a time visionary thinkers and designers synthe-
sized startling new miracle medications to cure slums, congestion, unpredictable change, and other maladies of cities. Some
went so far as to hope the prescriptions could dispose of
cities as if they themselves were diseases. The cures were en-
thusiastically embraced by university schools of architecture
and planning far and wide, and subsequently by politicians,
civil servants, developers, and bankers in customer cities. Master plans (both the name and the concept reeking of hubris)
accompanied by rules, regulations, standards, and subsidies
mandated the cures, which were known in their totality as
Modern City Planning.

Since human beings are the only city-building creatures, the
cures could not be tested first on animals. And since the medications were wholly synthetic and artificial, any potentially per-
nicious or lethal side-effects they might have were unknown.
Thus the prescriptions, in rapidly increased doses, were both
administered and taken strictly on faith.

John Sewell tells us here the tale of one city's experience
with this experiment and with its emerging side-effects, which
have included intractable city sprawl, enfeebled convenience
and vitality, waste of fertile land and energy resources, costly
infrastructures, and sacrifice of amenities from the past and
supports for community life.

What hit Toronto hit hundreds of cities. Indeed, samples of
Toronto's modern planning would look surprisingly at home
dropped alongside samples of modern planning in Glasglow
or Phoenix, Zagreb or Beijing. To be sure, bleak and brutal
agglomerations of low income housing projects in Toronto

pale beside such agglomerations in Chicago, and the city's
macerations from expressways are slight in comparison with
those borne by neighbouring cities across the border such as
Buffalo. But these are differences in scale and quantity of planning, not differences in kind. Toronto's postwar suburbs, which
are massive, are quite as baffling physically and incoherent socially as their counterparts anywhere, and fully as ecologically
destructive and as ill-suited to service by public transportation.

Sewell's meticulous and admirably calm account of how such
things came to be in Toronto transcends the tale of one city
and its particularities. If anything, it is all the more instructive
because the readily understandable scale does not boggle the
mind. Toronto does not present a caricature of the miracles
wrought by planning cures, nor does Sewell attempt to caricature them. This is a sober description of sober quackery. Not
to mince words, planners and their working colleagues did not
know what they were doing. Their remedies for slums, congestion, and other maladies were frauds.

Toronto, as it happens, withstood the great debilitating experiment fairly sturdily – more sturdily perhaps than any other
city in North America. Leaving aside its suburbs, the older city
displayed for the most part a strong immune system, so to
speak.

Why was this? As I see it, Toronto's immune system was for-
tified by grace of four important advantages denied to U.S.
cities that were otherwise not dissimilar. These differences have
their cautionary lessons too.

First, Canadian banks – unlike U.S. banks – did not adopt
the practice of 'redlining' various city neighbourhoods, desig-
nating property in them to be ineligible henceforth, for mort-
gages or other financial infusions. With a few exceptions Sewell
describes, old and modest Toronto neighbourhoods were not
automatically doomed to destruction, preceded by enforced
dilapidation and deterioration. As a result, many old Toronto
city neighbourhoods continued viable and, with passage of
time, they even grew stronger and increasingly desirable. These
neighbourhoods are not exceptional in Toronto as in so many
American cities; rather, they are the rule.

Second, although radical prejudices and discriminations infest Toronto too, these evils were not exacerbated and intensified by creation of racial ghettos. Creating ghettos actually requires much deliberate and calculated effort: for instance, redlining; well organized 'block-busting' on the part of ruthless developers or real-estate vultures; and contrived property-value panics to empty whites out of ghettos-to-be. These efforts were largely missing in Toronto, and when they were tried they were feeble and ineffectual, perhaps because they were not connived in by the authorities.

Third, the Canadian federal government has financed only one major automotive artery, the TransCanada Highway. Otherwise, the country lacks a federal highway program. Instead, city expressways (along with rural arteries) are artifacts of provincial and local governments. The planning by these bodies is no different from that by the u.s. federal government and states. The expressways planned for Toronto would have devastated the city, and they were difficult for citizens to oppose and halt before unredeemable damage was done. However, having had experience with such protests in both countries, I am of the opinion that saving Toronto from these juggernauts was less difficult and was accomplished more speedily than if the federal government and its largesse had been involved too.

Fourth, urban renewal schemes and programs were less destructive to Toronto than to cities across the border. The Canadian federal urban renewal agency came into being later than the u.s. agency it imitated and, as Sewell informs us, shut down operations sooner. While urban renewal lasted it was damaging, but it did not last long. That was because Canadian politicians soon perceived what a horrendous generator it was of civic dissentions and other nasty problems.

Now these four important advantages, in sum, consisted of virtues of omission – a mirror image, as it were, of sins of commission. Important though they were, they did not change the nature of modern planning itself, nor did they supply alternative techniques and goals.

A new generation of postmodern planners and policy-makers has begun emerging in Toronto. Their goals are different from those of their planning predecessors; so are their methods. Their aims are not as startling and splashy as the aims of modern planning; but neither are they as artificial, simple-minded, and incautious, and therein lies their hope. John Sewell is one of this new generation of policy-makers. He invites us here to share some of the homework he did, and thereby to begin grasping the profound difference between what was done by modern planning and what needs to be done now.

JANE JACOBS

Introduction

This book is about the coming of modern planning ideas to Canada and their influence on urban form in Toronto. These ideas were unchallenged – indeed they were lauded – for almost two decades after the Second World War. They were then rejected in the built-up areas of Toronto after a brief and decisive battle, but have continued to flourish at the edges of the city.

The details will certainly differ, but the broad struggle in Toronto between competing ideas of what a good city could be also happened in most other North American cities during the second half of the twentieth century. The story told here is a common one throughout the continent.

Most people tend to take built form for granted: the assumption seems to be, 'this is the way things are.' When it comes to the shape and form of places where we live, it is often difficult to recognize that, before the place had the shape it has, decisions were consciously made about what that shape was going to be. This is particularly true of new suburban neighbourhoods built since the 1960s: residents can't conceive of anyone thinking good communities should be planned differently. Rare is it for someone to question why suburbs are designed as they are, or why different approaches were not tried. In short, we assume the new parts of the city represent the best way to build cities.

But as is apparent to anyone who travels around Canadian and other North American cities, urban areas are divided into two distinct parts: one part has straight streets and short blocks, with dense development and little green space, and with housing and commercial uses mixed together, whether as corner stores or as shopping strips with apartments over stores; the

other part of the city is more open, streets more often than
not are curvy, development is much less intense, and there is a
clear distinction among shopping areas (shopping centres),
work areas, and residential areas.

The distinctions didn't happen by chance, as this book attempts to show using Toronto as the prime example. The newer
parts of Toronto were planned to be significantly different
from the older parts, although the reasons underlying the new
kinds of plans are often weak, flimsy, or downright unsubstantiated. The new style of city building, one might conclude,
seems to have emerged from half-baked ideas and has led to
the rise of many urban problems. These problems might easily
have been avoided if more thought had been given to a city
form that would best serve the needs of its residents.

The roots of the new ideas are found in the dream of the
ideal community. 'The suburbs,' writes Humphrey Carver, one
of Canada's most influential planners pushing for a new approach after the Second World War, 'are exactly what we asked
for. The suburbs are exactly what we've got' (Carver 1962, 3).
But Carver was hardly happy with the results:

As I looked around at the acreages of new housing, the stereotyped
forms were clearly being determined by the mortgaging system and
by the packaging of NHA [National Housing Act] incentives. There
must be, I felt, some principles of organic design that might help to
make places more hospitable to a good life. How could housespace
be arranged around the privacies of individuals and around the
structures of families? How could family houses be grouped together
so that social relationships in the suburbs would evolve spontane-
ously? And how could these housing groups and neighbours be
assembled into the forms of communities? How could the new
suburban landscape be made more passionate towards human life?
(Carver 1975, 115)

Carver's question was directed more at the urban form his
influence had spawned in the 1950s than at any urban form that
came before him. So too Lewis Mumford, one of the world's
leading urban critics in this century:

Instead of creating the regional city, the forces that automatically
pumped highways and motor cars and real estate developments into
the open country have produced the formless urban exudation.
Those who are using verbal magic to turn this conglomeration into
an organic entity are only fooling themselves. To call the resulting
mass Megalopolis, or to suggest that the change in special scale,
with swift transportation, in itself is sufficient to produce a new and
better urban form, is to overlook the complex nature of the city.
(Mumford 1961, 505)

Mumford expressed even more bitter reservations about the
new style:

Suburbia offers poor facilities for meeting, conversation, collective
debate, and common action – it favours silent comformity, not
rebellion or counter-attack. So suburbia has become the favoured
home of a new kind of absolutism: invisible but all-powerful.
(Mumford 1961, 513)

Neither man wished to blame the outcome on the new planning
ideas: better, in the twentieth-century mode, to blame it on large
economic forces or on the way society became the captive of
technology. Carver offered several different excuses:

The technological revolution put the family in the car and the
social revolution gave the family a house in the suburbs and all it
contains. (Carver 1962, 3)

   To a large extent the suburbs have been an accident, the
consequence of an elaborate interplay of forces in land speculation,
in traffic arrangements, and in the bid for consumer markets. (Carver
1975, 188)

Mumford was more specific about the role of the automobile
as the determining influence:

As soon as the motor car became common, the pedestrian scale of
the suburb disappeared and with it, most of its individuality and

charm. The suburb ceased to be a neighborhood unit: it became a
diffused low density mass. (Mumford 1961, 505)

It would be unfair to paint either Carver or Mumford as the
ogres of the piece: for many years they were the most percep-
tive critics of urban planning in North America. But it is only
with the waning of the modern movement that the pervasive-
ness of its assumptions become clear and it is possible to understand the mindset people living in mid-century carried
around as they looked at problems and opportunities.

What this book attempts to point out is where the new ideas
came from and how they became part of the fabric of city
building in Toronto. This approach helps to illuminate urban
political struggles as well as to provide some understanding of
why Toronto is the way it is at the end of the twentieth century. It also provides a reasonable approach for looking at
problems of urban form in other North American cities.

Many planners and architects have dreamed big dreams
about what cities should be. The modern movement in Toronto
is perhaps best summed up by an unnamed architect writing
in May 1940, in the *Journal* of the Royal Architectural Institute
of Canada (RAIC). Accompanying the five paragraphs is a photograph of an apartment building about a dozen stories high,
with the simple words under it: 'The Urban Way':

We have for many years been familiar with the spectacular architecture of commerce and industry. The skyscraper a thousand feet
high and the great industrial buildings have ceased to be more than
nine day wonders. The revolutionary architecture of a World's Fair
is accepted as an everyday phenomenon. We have created a new
aesthetic that has little to do with the past.

The great wonder of our times is, that the new beauty and the
new forms have not replaced archeology and sentimentality in the
buildings in which we live.

In these buildings the walls, the roof, the windows, and even the
ceilings have undergone no change in fundamentals for the past
five hundred years. House design is largely an exercise in archeology, and its criteria are those of this or that period in architectural

history rather than its ability to satisfy the requirements of modern
living. We make only grudging concession to those requirements for
no way has been found to incorporate them into our own part
without destruction of its prescribed harmony.

Against this sort of thing, architects today are setting their wills
and energy. The day of archaeological eclecticism is fast drawing to
a close. The new day promises a new beginning in which all the arts
and sciences of building will be used to the limit as they once were
in the great days of the cathedral builders.

It is with high purpose and certain hope that architects have
returned to those same great principles, which applied to the
building of man's habitations, may once again create for him a
ladder to the stars. (RAIC, *Journal,* May 1940, 74).

The dream of the new was a powerful one, but we now seem
able to give ourselves enough distance from it to propose our
own approaches to cities, ones that might be more modest, more
appropriate, and more amenable to the human condition.

The Shape of the City

1

Dreaming of a Better City

By the end of the nineteenth century the sentiment among intellectuals against the city had grown so clamorous that a serious search for alternatives began, one that lasted for almost a hundred years. By the middle of the twentieth century there was enough confidence among the new planners for the American, Clarence Stein, to issue this powerful call for the destruction of the old city and its replacement with the new:

Existing cities cannot fit the needs of this age without a complete rebuilding. It is not merely that the elements and the details of plan and mass urgently require new forms, but that the relationship of these to each other must be radically revised. For this, one must begin with a clean slate and a large one. Therefore it seems to me that the sane policy is first to direct our energy toward building new and complete communities from the ground up: that is to say on open land outside developed urban areas. This we should do until such time as we have adequately demonstrated, by contrast, how unworkable and wasteful are the obsolete patterns of the old cities, and how completely they demand replacement. It is futile to attempt this in a small piecemeal manner. Meanwhile, where attempts are made to redevelop our old cities, it must be done on an adequate scale to form New Towns or at least modern neighbourhoods within the old cities but to a pattern far different from the old ... Redevelopment will be valueless unless each scheme is part of a co-ordinated process that will ultimately make the old cities into New cities – modern cities. (Stein 1951, 218)

The notion that the city and its building required replacement by something more fitting for the times is at the root of modern culture. Three general strands of thought are pulled together under the rubric of modernism: a straightforward belief that cities are bad, in and of themselves; a sense that cities are unhealthy – physically, socially, aesthetically, and morally; and a feeling that cities mitigate against a good family life. These ideas found expression in Western thought from the sixteenth century onward, and fell on fertile ground in thought and deed in the twentieth century.

The general anti-urban sentiment is captured well in Morton and Lucia White's 1962 work, *The Intellectual versus the City*. The tradition of hating the city has a long and pervasive history on this side of the Atlantic Ocean – anti-urban sentiments can be found in American writers as diverse as Ralph Waldo Emerson, Herman Melville, Nathaniel Hawthorne, Henry Adams, Henry James, and John Dewey, and was summed up admirably by Henry Ford's pithy salespitch for his automobiles: 'We shall solve the City Problem by leaving the city' (White 1977, 201). The Whites conclude, 'just because different intellectuals have disliked the city for so many different reasons, it is unlikely that one simple hypothesis will provide "the" explanation of why American thinkers have found the city objectionable.' One branch of objectors might be labelled primitivists, for their love of the unsettled countryside; the other, sophisticates, who could not tolerate the city's great sense of muddle and excitement. Together, these thrusts managed to deny ground to almost anyone who thought the city had some values worth praising. Jane Jacobs notes that even such an ardent defender of the city as Lewis Mumford denigrated it, applying names to its various manifestations such as 'Megolopolis, Tyrannopolis, Nekroplis, a monstrosity, a tyranny, a living death' (Jacobs 1961, 20–1)

That American sentiment spilled over into Canada. Few Canadian intellectuals had good things to say about cities: painters and writers took to the woods in their search for the meaningful life, in the process creating a compelling body of work outside cities. Rural scenes and small towns might be fit subjects for the artist, but the crowning glory for the most serious painter was a turbulent river, a wind-swept island, or the lonely bush. In the early twentieth century the Group of Seven raised such a vision to become a national icon, one that was hardly ruffled by the painters of the 1930s whose themes sometimes focused on urban workers. Much of the Canadian identity since that time has swirled around the images the Group created.

Apparently Canadian artists felt cities were places to leave as quickly as they could. William Wordsworth could stand on

Westminster Bridge, view the city, and say:

> Earth has not anything to show more fair:
> Dull would he be of soul who could pass by
> A sight so touching in its majesty:
> This city now doth, like a garment wear
> The beauty of the morning: silent, bare,
> Ships, towers, domes, theatres and temples lie
> Open unto the fields and to the sky:
> All bright and glittering in the smokeless air.

But there was no corresponding sentiment in Canadian verse. This is not the place to undertake a complete review of Canadian literature or art, but a few examples make the point: the anti-urban bias in Canada has deep roots and a strong tradition. One of the few times a city is mentioned before 1925 is in Archibald Lampman's poem, 'The City of the End of Things.' It is a city of evil horror full of noise, fire, and darkness:

> Through its grim depths re-echoing
> And all its weary height of walls,
> With measured roar and iron ring,
> The inhuman music lifts and falls ...
>
> All its grim grandeur, tower and hall,
> Shall be abandoned utterly,
> And into rust and dust shall fall
> From century to century;
> Nor ever living thing shall grow,
> Nor trunk of tree, nor blade of grass ...
> (Atwood 1982, 36–7)

Precious little Canadian verse acknowledges the existence of cities or city experiences, and, when it does, most frequently it follows Lampman's negative example. In the 1982 *New Oxford Book of Canadian Verse*, only twenty-one poems have references to cities, many disdainful. Poets such as Dennis Lee, Raymond Souster, and Miriam Waddington, who seem to begin with the assumption that the city is not an enemy, are exceptions. Dennis Lee, in his collection *New Canadian Poets, 1970–85*, included only fourteen poems making even the vaguest of references to cities.

Margaret Atwood, arguably Canada's most published author, castigates cities in virtually everything she writes. Toronto figures largely in her novel *Life before Man*, but it is a city that is faceless, devoid of empathy or meaning, and the novel closes with the leading female character wishing Toronto did not exist. Atwood ends *The Journals of Susanna Moodie* on the St Clair Avenue bus in December:

> I am the old woman
> sitting across from you on the bus
> ...
> Turn, look down:
> there is no city;
> this is the centre of a forest
> your place is empty. (Atwood 1970, 61)

In an afterword Atwood notes: 'She makes her final appearance in the present as an old woman on a Toronto bus who reveals the city as an unexplored, threatening wilderness.'

Stephen Leacock set the tone for many Canadian authors with *Sunshine Sketches*, singing the joys of the small town. The book concludes in a large railway station as the businessman dreams of an escape from the confusing city back to the security of Mariposa:

> It leaves the city every day about five o'clock in the evening, the train for Mariposa.
>
> Strange you did not know of it, though you come from the little town – or did, long years ago.
>
> Odd that you never knew, in all these years, that the train was there every afternoon, puffing up steam in the city station, and that you might have boarded it any day and gone home. No, not 'home' – of course you couldn't call it 'home' now; 'home' means that big red sandstone house of yours in the costlier part of the city. 'Home'

means, in a way, this Mausoleum Club where you sometimes talk
with me of the times that you had as a boy in Mariposa.

...

But if you have half forgotten Mariposa, and long since lost the
way to it, you are only like the greater part of the men here in this
Mausoleum Club in the city. Would you believe it that practically
every one of them came from Mariposa once upon a time, and that
there isn't one of them that doesn't sometimes dream in the dull
quiet of the long evening here in the club, that some day he will go
back and see the place. (Leacock 1947, 260–2)

Alice Munro and Margaret Laurence have followed the same
course, concentrating their finest work in small-town locales.
Robertson Davies remarks in *The Manticore*, the middle book of
the Deptford trilogy, 'If Deptford was my Arcadia, Toronto was
a place of no such comfort' (Davies 1972, 103).

In spite of great promises, Davies shies away from a full-
blown urban setting. Davies has no great hatred towards cities (as
is shown, for instance, by Mordecai Richler's Duddy Kravitz,
who castigates Montreal from the mountain), but he usually
locates action indoors, in a protected environment. Virtually
the whole of *The Rebel Angels* occurs in a series of interior
spaces: stairs, a chapel, an eatery, laboratories, and other assorted
rooms – perhaps not inappropriate settings for a Jungian.

Hugh MacLennan and Morley Callaghan are two significant
exceptions in an otherwise anti-urban Canadian writers' world.
For both, the city is as natural a place for a character to find
definition as any rock in the woods. MacLennan puts Kathleen
Tallard in a chair by a window in *Two Solitudes*:

Her old sense of the city's wholeness returned to her: it gripped her
feelings and imagination the way she remembered it from girlhood.
She heard the streetcars banging across the nearest intersection, the
intermittent sound of motor horns, the faint shuffling of thousands
of moving feet. The crowds passing under the window seemed all
about her. She stretched out her long legs as far as they would go.
The stretched toes touched, and her arms went to behind her head

as her eyes closed. She smiled. It was good to be peaceful again, to be one's self; it was wonderful to be unknown in the crowd. (MacLennan 1945, 120).

The Watch That Ends the Night praises Montreal:

It is a curious city, Montreal, and in this story I keep returning to the fact that it is. Strangers never understand its inner nature, and immigrant families, even from other parts of Canada, can live here two generations without coming to know it in its bones. I am absolutely certain that Montreal is the subtlest and most intricate city in North America. (MacLennan 1959, 238)

Callaghan takes the same positive approach. Kip Caley, the unreformed bank robber in *More Joy in Heaven*, is accompanied by a priest at his mother's deathbed. The priest starts the conversation:

'I suppose you've been all over the country, city after city, always on the move, eh?' A kind of longing came into his voice. His head tilted over on one side as if he were dreaming. Puzzled, Kipp said, 'You like big cities, eh?'
'I often think I'd like to see great stretches of country rolling by,' he said. 'But I like crowds. I like to see swarms of people. I'd like to get to New York. I'd like to see thousands of faces on the streets drifting by.' (Callaghan 1966, 137)

But the more dominant theme is expressed by a lesser known writer, Bertram Warr, writing in 1970:

Though the cities straddle the land like giants, holding us away,
we know they will topple some day,
and will lie over the land giving off gases.
But a wind will spring up to carry the smells away
and the earth will suck off the liquids and the crumbling flesh,
and on the bleached bones, when the sun shines,
we shall begin to build. (Atwood 1982, 195)

While the city may have failed Canadian writers as a locus of the imagination, most Canadians were city dwellers from the mid nineteenth century on. Commentators looked at this real world and concluded the city was a place that threatened health.

Certainly there was plenty of dirt and soot: it poured from factory chimneys where coal was the common fuel, from trains criss-crossing the cities and the countryside, and from the hearths and furnaces of every home. Sewage systems left much to be desired, including a pungent odour. As cities grew, these problems intensified. Laws were passed – beginning in England with the Public Health Act of 1875 – to ensure a standard of urban design that was expected to help alleviate health problems. Thus, one law required streets to be of a certain width, often straight, creating space between buildings to help control the spread of cholera and permit access by vehicles to remove night soil and garbage. These were the real beginnings of modern city planning.

Questions of physical health became intertwined with questions of social and moral well-being. Urban reform in Canada, at least as expressed in the stewardship of William Howland, Toronto's reform mayor elected in 1885, was mostly an attack on organized sin: 'the saloon, the gambling den, the house of prostitution, even the theatre. [Reformers] were convinced that vice was so much a fact of city life that it menaced the national destiny' (Artibise and Stetler 1977, 371).

These kinds of sentiments were not wholly of a Canadian origin: cities throughout the developing world were seen to be subject to the same pressures, answerable to the same shortfalls. As one author notes in an English context:

Much of the sharpest criticism had to do with the material and physical hardships that stemmed from the clearly excessive crowding of too many people in too little space in the areas inhabited by ordinary city dwellers. The seeming inability of many urban men and women not only to live reasonably long and healthy lives of their own but also to raise adequate numbers of off-spring was a basic source of deep anxiety for urban critics during almost all of the period. Fears that pertained to sanitation, housing, death rates,

and birth rates were closely linked to the belief that the big cities
undermined the bases of religion and morality, that they mitigated
against stable families and other forms of primary social control,
and that they manifested far more than their fair share of vice,
crime, and the propensity to revolt. A less pervasive but nonetheless
quite powerfully expressed worry was that cities – if only because of
the sheer ugliness that seemed to disfigure so many of them – were
producing a race of men and women who possessed a woefully
underdeveloped sensitivity to beauty and an equally deficient
capacity for creative originality of any sort. (Lees 1985, 306)

Questions of morality also seemed indistinguishable from
questions of social welfare and health. Those latter areas attracted their share of reformers at the turn of the century,
notably Dr Charles Hastings in Toronto and the Rev. J.S.
Woodsworth in Winnipeg. Hastings was the medical officer of
health for Toronto from 1910 to 1929, and he pressed an ambitious program of preventative measures to improve health
and well-being: water treatment, sewage treatment, government-
sponsored housing, and municipally owned abattoirs. He was a
driving force behind the implementation of new planning ideas
in housing for working people (see chapter 2). Planning, health,
and municipal reform went hand in hand: under his leadership,
Toronto had the most progressive public health program on
the continent.

Before becoming a national political figure, Woodsworth
took his role as a clergyman to mean he should help the immigrant and the poor. He was optimistic about the positive
effects of physical changes on the soul of the urban dweller
and, in his 1912 book *My Neighbour*, he writes: 'These changed
ideals of living will be reflected in our customs and also inevitably react upon our characters. The highly developed social
man will be psychologically, ethically and spiritually far in advance of his ancestors who had learned only to live to themselves' (MacInnis 1953, 74).

Concerns for a healthier city found expression at the turn of
the century in the City Beautiful movement. Daniel Burnham
proposed a new plan for Chicago in 1909, hoping 'to restore to

the city a lost visual and aesthetic harmony, thereby creating the physical prerequisite for the emergence of a harmonious social order' (Hall 1988, 179). The plan consisted of a new civic centre as well as new boulevards clearing away the slums (reminiscent of the plans of Haussmann in Paris a half century earlier), giving the city a new sense of cohesion and purpose. As Peter Hall notes, 'Its very confusion of social objectives and purely aesthetic means was, apparently, the quality that endeared it to the middle classes' (179).

Several examples of the movement's work are still extant in Canada, of which the communities of Lindenlea in Ottawa and Hydrostone in Halifax are prominent. Both were the work of Thomas Adams, a British planner who served as secretary of the Garden City Association from 1901 to 1906 during the construction of the first Garden City, Letchworth; served as first president of the Town Planning Institute, established in 1913; came to Canada in 1914 for a decade; then left for the United States. Lindenlea was designed for a fresh patch of land being appended to the urban fabric of Ottawa; Hydrostone was planned for the Richmond neighbourhood in Halifax, which had been devastated by the Halifax explosion in 1917. Both are based on a substantially modified grid road form, using diagonal and curved streets to emphasize vistas and greenery.

In Toronto, proponents of the City Beautiful formed themselves into the Civic Improvements Committee in 1911 and drafted a plan for Toronto's downtown immediately preceding the Great War. The plans came to naught: the notion that physical change would provoke a significant improvement in the lives of city dwellers had not yet taken hold. Yet it was apparent that the link was of great interest to city planners. Similar plans resurfaced in the late 1920s, with the same intent: destruction of slum areas and their replacement with beautifully designed streets expected to improve the lives of city dwellers. It was as though planners seized upon the Halifax explosion as having accomplished a greater good by providing an opportunity to begin again, and wished to export that idea to other cities. Those plans, however, never became more than a gleam in the planner's eye.

Plan for Lindenlea, Ottawa. The original caption when first published in 1919 was 'Lindenlea, the Ottawa Housing Commission's development, has been planned along economic lines to give ideal results at low cost.' Most noticeable is the attempt to create a street pattern other than grid.

The Contract Record, August 1991

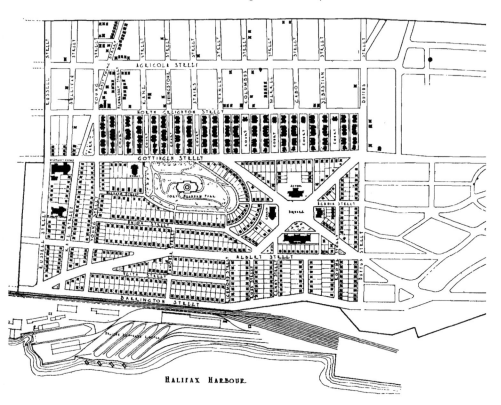

HALIFAX HARBOUR

Richmond neighbourhood, Halifax. The area completely destroyed by the
Halifax explosion lay between North Creighton Street and Barrington Street.
Thomas Adams used this opportunity to dispense with the grid road plan
between Gottingen and Barrington streets in favour of diagonal and gently
curving streets. The transition to the abutting grid system, between Gottingen
and North Creighton streets, is laced with green strips in the middle of the
road. Public Archives of Nova Scotia

Opposite: John Lyle's 1911 plan for the Civic Improvement Committee shows
the City Beautiful movement at its most cocky: a street (Federal Avenue) is
carved out of the existing blocks to lead grandly to a set of new municipal
buildings set just to the west of (and eclipsing) Toronto City Hall, which had
opened only a dozen years before. City of Toronto Archives

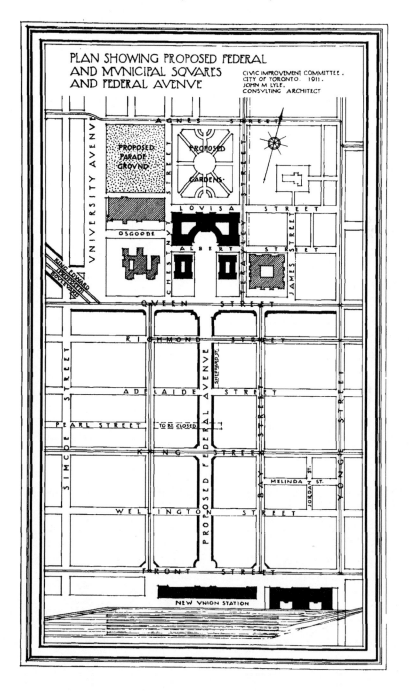

PLAN SHOWING PROPOSED FEDERAL
AND MVNICIPAL SQVARES
AND FEDERAL AVENVE

CIVIC IMPROVEMENT COMMITTEE.
CITY OF TORONTO. 1911.
JOHN M. LYLE.
CONSVLTING ARCHITECT

PROPOSED
PARADE
GROVND.

PROPOSED
GARDENS·

OSGOODE

NEW VNION STATION

There was a third strain to critical thought and comment about cities. Not only did the very existence of cities raise enmity, not only did many question their physical and moral influence on human beings, but questions arose whether cities were appropriate places in which to raise a family.

Since the mid seventeenth century there had been a growing criticism that traditional city patterns were not satisfactory for maintaining a family. On the one hand, work/residence relationships, hitherto in the same structure, now began to separate under the pressures of increasing industrialization as the role of the artisan declined. On the other hand, the masculine perception of women underwent a radical change.

Robert Fishman argues that the separation of work and residence was reinforced by the evangelical ideal of the family: 'The city was not just crowded, dirty and unhealthy; it was immoral. Salvation itself depended on separating the woman's sacred world of family and children from the profane metropolis.' At the same time, the husband had to attend to daily work, 'for hard work and success were also Evangelical virtues – and business life required rapid personal access to that great beehive of information which was London. This was the problem, and suburbia was to be the ultimate solution' (Fishman 1987, 38). The solution to the tension was to remove the woman and her children from the city and place them in a country setting, or to attempt some kind of mixture of city and country to obtain the best of both worlds.

The proposed mixture of city and country was of course not new. Houses had been built in the country for city dwellers for many centuries, although exactly when and why this phenomenon began is difficult to pin down. Mumford is unable to put an exact date on when a country house became a suburban house, but he suggests something new began to happen in the twelfth and thirteenth centuries, just as the medieval walled city was at its culmination and walls were constantly being moved to accommodate new growth. These trends were noticeable in Florence in 1172 (Mumford 1961, 312ff), but it was not until a century or two later that the elements of the new form were more apparent:

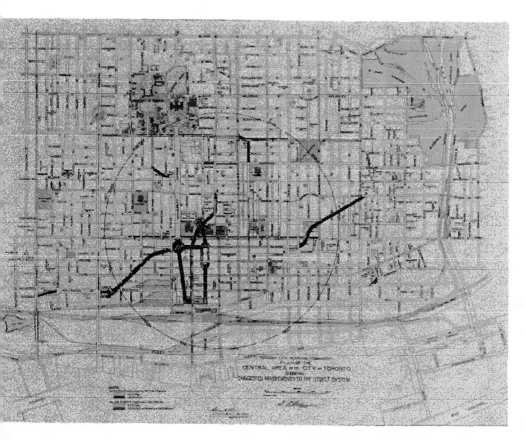

This plan, eighteen years later, goes several steps further than Lyle's plan, creating a new intersection north of Queen, as well as several new diagonal streets that attempt to pierce the downtown grid. The one part of the plan that was implemented is the extension of University Avenue south of Queen Street. City of Toronto Archives

As early as the thirteenth century, indeed, Villani reported that the land for a circle of three miles around Florence was occupied by rich estates with costly mansions; and Venetian families were not behind in their villas on the Brenta. From the beginning, the privileges and delights of suburbanism were reserved largely for the upper class; so that the suburb might almost be described as the collective urban form of the country house – the house in the park – as the suburban way of life is so largely a derivative of the relaxed, playful, goods-consuming aristocratic life that developed out of the rough, bellicose, strenuous existence of the feudal stronghold. (Mumford 1961, p. 484)

Mumford also suggests a different image at the root of this new form, 'a sort of rural isolation ward' (487), as he attributes the growth of the suburb to an attempt to escape the dreaded plague in the thirteenth century. But he takes the idea further, suggesting this new development is infused with different values from those traditionally found in the city:

Let me emphasize the demand for space, which changed the whole scale of urban planning once the protective fortification ceased to be essential for security. Whatever else the suburb has stood for, it has demanded the enlargement of the areas of open green and garden, as proper appurtenances of the city. What only kings could demand once, was now the prerogative of every commoner who could get hold of the land itself. (Mumford 1961, 488)

The crowded, polluted industrial city of the eighteenth and nineteenth century, Mumford claims, demanded that people look for comfortable places in the country, and new city additions, new suburbs, took on appropriate forms in contrast to the settled city. Since urban growth occurred on the periphery of the city, the suburbs became identified with the spreading city and were no longer a refuge from the city itself.

John Nash's 1812 plan for Regent's Park in London stressed that very element, setting elegant houses in a large country-like park. The 1853 plan for Llewellyn Park, an early railway suburb in New Jersey twelve miles east of Manhattan, had the

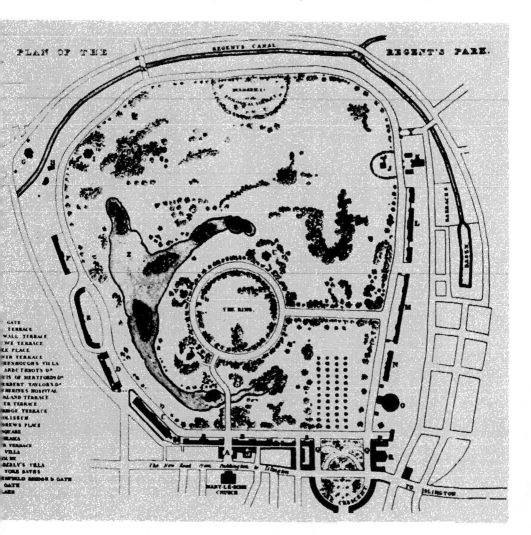

Regent's Park, London. John Nash, 1812. The park is so extensive that the residential buildings on the edges of the circular promenade are hardly noticeable.

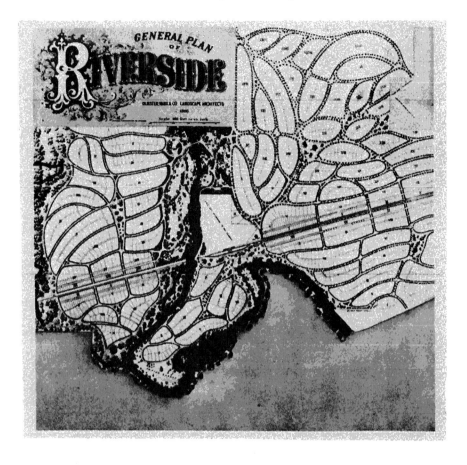

Riverside, Chicago. Frederick Law Olmsted, 1869. Olmsted rejected the grid
plan as 'too stiff and formal,' and relied on heavy plantings to make the site
seem more park-like.

same intent, setting one hundred villa sites around a fifty acre communal park. Later plans such as Frederick Law Olmsted's 1869 Riverside, outside Chicago, and Garden City in New York in the same year attempted more comprehensive approaches to houses developed in a countrified setting, but both ran into substantial setbacks in the construction stage and were never completed (Stern 1981, 24).

Olmsted saw the new form he was helping to develop as not a step back from the city, but such a giant step forward in residential amenity that it would replace the importance of the city centre itself: 'It would appear then, that the demands of suburban life ... are not to be a regression from, but an advance upon, those which are characteristic of town life, and that no great town can long exist without great suburbs' (Sutton 1971, 295). He favoured a curved rather than a straight street because of the effect: 'Gracefully curved lines, generous spaces and the absence of sharp corners, the idea being to suggest and imply leisure, contemplativeness and happy tranquillity' (Sutton 1971, 300).

These projects, and others like them including Toronto's Rosedale (modelled on Riverside), were built to be a preserve of the moneyed elite. They were never advanced as alternatives to the whole of the urban form. They were limited urban additions in a very careful style. Their function was not so much to provide an alternative as to complement the existing city.

The idea of a new style, however complementary, gained impetus when yoked with the changing religious climate. It fit well with the new role men had appropriated for women as the family member responsible for child-rearing and family harmony. Women had to be put where they could protect the young from the rigours – perhaps even the problems – of the city, thus dictating a separation between where people worked and where they lived. That separation was accompanied by other opportunities of the growing middle class for an exclusive existence, particularly the opportunity to remove themselves from the lower classes. Fishman writes: 'The emergence of suburbia required a total transformation of urban values: not only a reversal in meanings of core and periphery, but a separation of work and family life and the creation of new forms of urban space that would be both class segregated and wholly residential' (Fishman 1987, 8).

Not everyone was a believer in the new direction as it tried to establish itself in the nineteenth century. One critic noted, in a prescient sentence for 1876: 'A modern suburb is a place which is neither one thing nor the other, which has neither the advantage of the town nor the open freedom of the country, but manages to combine in a nice equality of proportion the disadvantages of both' (Edwards 1981, 223). But many more took the changes to heart, and the idea of the new suburb was treated as a valid way to challenge the city's very being. The model dwelling societies formed in England in midcentury provided homes for 60,000 families by 1900 (Buder 1990, 71). The search for the ideal community spawned many new urban concepts – Edward Bellamy in *Looking Backward*, William Morris in *News from Nowhere*, and the writings of H.G. Wells, to name the most prominent.

In the midst of the English urban reform movement was the clerk/accountant Ebenezer Howard, who outlined his synthesis of ideas for a new city, a garden city, in a speech in 1893 (Buder 1990, chap. 5). The interest provoked by the speech led to the publication of his ideas in 1898. Howard proposed, as Mumford writes in a 1945 preface to the republished work, 'a marriage of town and country, of rustic health and sanity and activity and urban knowledge, urban technical facility, urban political co-operation' (Howard 1965, 34). The new city would consist of a central urban core of 1000 acres carefully planned to incorporate grand avenues, boulevards, cultural facilities, and a central park, surrounded by 5000 acres of agricultural land. The population of the garden city would be 32,000. But Howard argued for more than just a new plan: he wanted to lead a crusade for a new kind of city. The first edition of his book was entitled *Tomorrow: A Peaceful Path to Real Reform*, and the opening page cited a verse from J.R. Lowell's 'The Present Crisis':

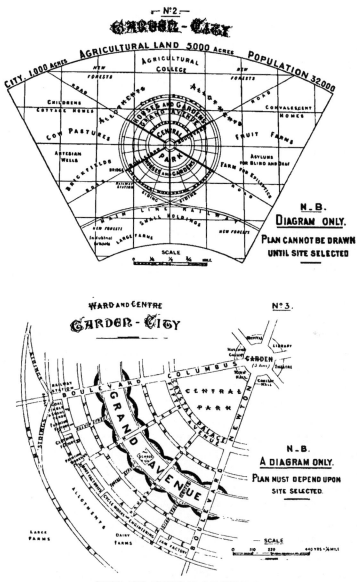

Garden City plans. Ebenezer Howard, 1899. The top plan shows the general
layout of the community; the bottom a detail of a portion of the city,
with uses noted, and streets named after those who 'invented' new kinds of
physical worlds. Howard 1965

New occasions teach new duties
Time makes ancient good uncouth,
They must upward still and onward
Who would keep abreast of truth.
Lo, before us, gleam her campfires,
We ourselves must pilgrims be,
Launch our 'Mayflower' and steer boldly
Through the desperate winter sea.
Nor attempt the future's portal
With the Past's blood-rusted key.

The challenge was to find the way out of the failures of the
Victorian age and set sail for the new world. What had been
done in the past in the way of city building would not be
appropriate for the future age – thus the disdain for 'the Past's
blood-rusted key' – but instead some other way must be found
by the seekers of the new truth.

By 1902 the title had been toned down to *Garden Cities of Tomorrow*, and Lowell's poem was no longer at the beginning.
Instead, a quote from J.R. Green's *Short History of the English
People* was used, achieving the same intention: 'New forces,
new cravings, new aims, which had been silently gathering
beneath the crust of reaction, burst suddenly into view.' Howard
still saw his role as providing the world with a blueprint for
cities that would fit the modern age.

The new urban reformers were infused with religious intent
since they expected the ideal city of the future would play a
large part in the shaping of modern man. For Howard, the
New Jerusalem would solve age-old human problems and restore a proper relationship between human beings and the
land, one that had been vitiated by cities:

Yes, the key to the problem how to restore the people to the land –
that beautiful land of ours, with its canopy of sky, the air that blows
upon it, the sun that warms it, the rain and dew that moisten it –
the very embodiment of Divine love for man – is indeed a Master
Key, for it is the key to a portal through which, even when scarce
ajar, will be seen to pour a flood of light on the problems of intem-

perance, of excessive toil, of restless anxiety, of grinding poverty –
the true limits of Governmental interference, ay, and the relations
of man to the Supreme Power. (Howard 1965, 44)

The solution proposed is a city that mixes the town and the
country:

There are in reality not only, as is constantly assumed, two alternatives – town life and country life – but a third alternative, in which
all the advantages of the most energetic and active town life, with all
the beauty and delight of the country, may be secured in perfect
combination; and the certainty of being able to live this life will be
the magnet which will produce the effect for which we are all
striving – the spontaneous movement of the people from our
crowded cities to the bosom of our kindly mother earth, at once
the source of life, of happiness, of wealth, and of power. (Howard
1965, 45)

The present city is rejected out of hand:

The well-lit streets are a great attraction, especially in winter, but the
sunlight is being more and more shut out, while the air is so vitiated
that the fine public buildings, like the sparrows, rapidly become
covered with soot, and the very statues are in despair. Palatial
edifices and fearful slums are the strange, complementary features
of modern cities. (Howard 1965, 47)

The new city, by contrast, is far superior:

I will undertake, then, to show how in 'Town-country' equal, nay
better, opportunities of social intercourse may be enjoyed than
are enjoyed in any crowded city, while yet the beauties of nature
may encompass and enfold each dweller therein; how higher
wages are compatible with reduced rents and rates; how abundant
opportunities for employment and bright prospects for advance-
ment may be secured for all; how capital may be attracted and
wealth created; how the most admirable sanitary conditions may
be ensured; how beautiful homes and gardens may be seen on
every hand; how the bounds of freedom may be widened, and

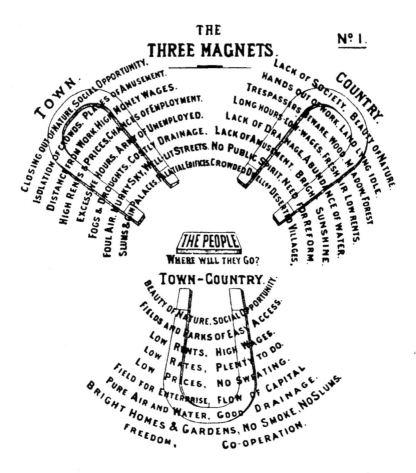

Howard's three magnets. One of the first bits of development puffery for
what the new community would offer its residents. Howard 1965

yet all the best results of concert and co-operation gathered in by a happy people. (Howard 1965, 48)

The opportunity, argues Howard, is to move people from the crowded city to the open country: 'it has been shown that an organized, migratory movement from over-developed, high-priced land to comparatively raw and unoccupied land, will enable all who desire it to live this life of equal freedom and opportunity; and a sense of the possibility of a life on earth at once orderly and free dawns upon the heart and mind' (Howard 1965, 125).

Howard's book gives eloquent voice to values that gained ascendancy in North America in the latter part of the twentieth century, values that were expressed by many suburban planners, developers, and housebuyers: lower densities are better; using farmland on the edge of the city will result in lower house prices; and suburbia gives freedom.

Several decades later, the American architect Frank Lloyd Wright took the same missionary approach to city building as did Howard. He also engaged in direct assault on the city, although from a somewhat different perspective:

This society of ours has overbuilt and now persists in over inhabiting cities – a wholly inorganic basis for survival now shamefully battening upon sources of extrinsic production; senselessly increasing production for the sake of more production ... The old city, already distinctly dated by its own excess, is only further outmoded by every forced increase. (Wright 1958, 38)

In no planning which the old city has received has modern spacing been based fairly enough upon the new time scale of modern mobilization – the human being no longer on his feet or seated in a trap behind a horse or two, but in his motorcar or going in his plane ... machinery has brought us no alternative plan. (Wright 1958, 53)

The old form of city, except as a market, has little or nothing substantial to give modern civilization except wagery, little or nothing above the belt – except degeneration. (Wright 1958, 26)

Broadacres city. Frank Lloyd Wright. Wright's caption reads: 'Typical
street view at civic centre with new type vertical body car and helicopter
taxi in flight. Street lights, seen at intervals low on curbs, are placed alter-
nately opposite to each other. In distance, universal (nonsectarian) cathedral. Tower at right, combination apartments and offices.' What is not at
first obvious is that this view depicts the heart of the city's downtown.

Broadacres city. Frank Lloyd Wright. Wright's caption reads: 'Patterns of cultivation mingling with good buildings. Helicopter seen in foreground and beyond, automatic overpass enabling continuous, uninterrupted traffic four ways.'
This, apparently, is suburban Broadacres, with the emphasis on uninterrupted
travel rather than achieving a sense of place. c 1958 FLWRIGHT FDN

The solution for Wright, like Howard, was a new kind of city based on a closer attachment to the ground, with much lower residential densities. He called his concept Broadacre City:

Of all the underlying forces working toward emancipation of the city dweller, most important is the gradual re-awakening of the primitive instincts of the agrarian ... uniting desirable features of the city with the freedom of the ground in natural happy union: such reintegration as here called Broadacre City ... We have earned the good right to speak of this city of tomorrow, the city of Democracy, indulging in no double-talk, as the City of Broad Acres. (Wright 1958, 64, 74)

In regard to the need to spread people out, he broaches no dissent: 'Any wise recognition and definition of freedom under Democracy must say that ultimate human satisfactions no longer depend upon but are destroyed by density of population' (Wright 1958, 70).

The Living City, the book from which these quotes are taken, is a mishmash of ideas and reflections, and it is not easy to get a comprehensive picture of the Broadacre vision. Apparently it will consist of homes spread out on one-acre lots, with 'patterns of cultivation mingling with good buildings.' But the exact nature of the execution seems less important to Wright than a castigation of present urban forms and the need for new cities to express the new, modern values – the same seductive approach used by Howard:

The means to live a more loveable life now demands a more livable city. This Broadacre concept of city planning simply means that any building in any place, of whatever kind, is concerned first with the new sense of space in spaciousness and of the nature appropriate to purpose and material and tools. (Wright 1958, 152)

Perhaps of greatest import is the houseform Wright developed: the one-and-a-half-storey ranch-style house, which for more than half a century has been the mainstay of the modern suburb, the prototypical suburban house.

The visions of Howard and Wright share three characteris-

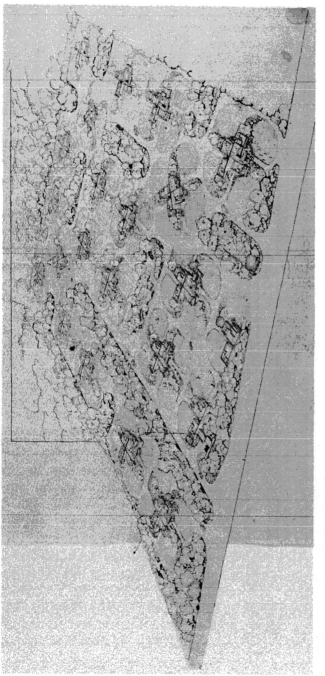

Broadacre houses. Frank Lloyd Wright. The sketch shows quadruple housing, with four units on two acres, so each segment of the house has one-half acre as a lawn or garden. c 1958 FLWRIGHT FDN

tics: a disdain for the city as it then stood and the longing for a
new experimental city form that will replace it; a desire to
forge a new link to the land, to wed together the city and the
country in some mystical way; and a certain knowledge that
whatever the new city would be like, residential densities would
be much lower than in existing cities.

The Swiss architect Le Corbusier took these ideas and turned
them inside out. He wanted, as the Goodman brothers say, to
'bring the greenbelt into the city itself' (Goodman 1947, 27).
Rather than building the new city on the edge of what already
existed, Le Corbusier in his Ville radieuse scheme called for a
destruction of the congested, interlayered city and its replacement with soaring towers separated by wide roadways and expanses of green space. One critic notes, 'The plan is extremely
simple and elegant: either to demolish the existing chaos or
start afresh on a new site; lay out in levels highways and tram-
ways radiating from the centre; on these erect a few towering
skyscrapers every 400 meters at the subway stations; and ring
this new opened-out centre with large apartment houses for
residences, a "cité jardin," the French kind of Garden City'
(Goodman 1947, 43).

Hall thinks Le Corbusier approached the new order with
considerable ambiguity and confusion. 'To save itself, every
great city must rebuild its centre,' Le Corbusier advocated (Hall
1988, 209). And the planning was too important to be left to
mere residents: 'The harmonious city must first be planned by
experts who understand the science of urbanism. They must
work out their plans in total freedom from partisan pressures
and special interests; once their plans are formulated, they
must be implemented without opposition' (Hall 1988, 210).

The technique proposed by Le Corbusier was somewhat
different from that advocated by Howard, who suggested
building on the outskirts of existing cities, but the aim was the
same. Le Corbusier wanted to destroy the old city and replace
it with something much more ordered, less congested, and,
although in giant towers, less dense. The continuity of the old,
or even a respect for the past, found no favour here. The tall
towers, while at great variance with the smaller scales suggested

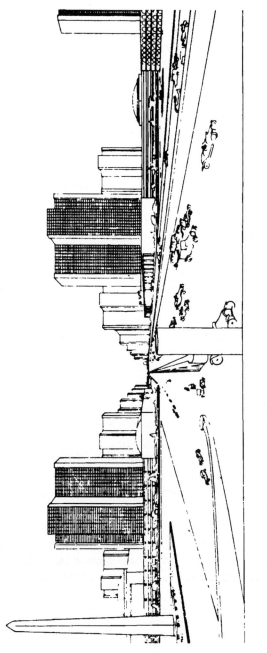

La Ville radieuse, streetscape. Le Corbusier's vision, now seventy years old, has been cast in concrete in many cities on both sides of the Atlantic, although perhaps without the roads being quite so wide, without the vista being quite so deep.

by Howard and Wright, encapsulated the excitement of new technology, one of the driving forces for humans in the twentieth century.

One Canadian architect, A.S. Mathers, caught the promise of Le Corbusier's approach in a 1940 speech:

The technique of the tall building can be used to release the ground with its grass and trees, for the use of the city dweller. The universal adoption of this principle in urban planning and housing would have most spectacular results. When you consider that it is possible as has been demonstrated by Corbusier in Paris, to achieve densities as high as 400 per acre, by using buildings 150 feet high and occupying only 12 per cent of the site, leaving 88 per cent of the entire area for parks and other purposes adjacent to the buildings, not a mile away. The country is thereby brought into the city and you have the ideal of all town planners, the 'city of green' with no suburbs. The town ends abruptly at the farm lands surrounding it. We come back to the medieval concept of the town. (Mathers 1940, 71)

Howard, Wright, and Le Corbusier gained their prominence not by being unusual, but by providing leadership for a willing host of followers. Of course, the reality rarely turned out to be as enticing as the idea: a clutch of high rises surrounded by green open space is hardly a return to the medieval town. Hall notes sarcastically, 'The evil that Le Corbusier did lives after him.'

In 1904, for instance, Letchworth was planned just outside London, to be built on Howard's model. Indeed, the sponsoring company was entitled the First Garden City, Ltd. Architects Barry Parker and Raymond Unwin were retained to create a plan for the 4500 acre site, but in the end it was a very mixed success. Howard's ideas for innovative land tenure and rents were abandoned; the enterprise had difficulty attracting sufficient capital and commercial businesses; agricultural principles were generally ignored; and construction was never fully completed (Buder 1990, chap. 7). What was built didn't hang together. One commentator notes: 'The result is neither an

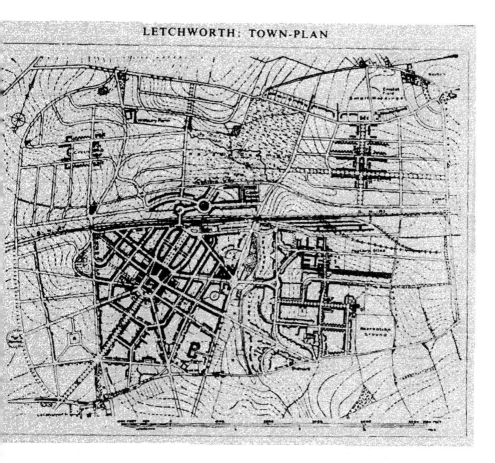

LETCHWORTH: TOWN-PLAN

Letchworth, London. Parker and Unwin, 1904. The plan incorporates, in modified form, Howard's fan-shaped road pattern (in the bottom left-hand corner), as well as an intermeshing of agricultural uses as a part of the town.

ordered, planned city nor an agglutinated village ... It can be argued that the problems that would beset large-scale suburban planning in the 20th century were planted at Letchworth: philanthropy was rejected in favour of a capitalism which brought with it the kind of land speculation and market-based aesthetics all too familiar to the post-war era' (Stern 1981, 58). Hampstead followed, but its success rested more with architecture than with planning.

More often, the ideas were seized by others for imaginative and successful implementation. In the 1920s Clarence Stein made a serious attempt to define an urban form that expressed the new planning ideas in Sunnyside Gardens, a seventy-seven-acre area in Queens, New York City. In keeping with the new thinking, the predominant element was the large scale of the conception, with individual elements (including houses) subservient to the overall plan. Houses are set in blocks surrounding (or surrounded by) gardens and open space, providing a new and powerful urban experience that continues to have an impressive effect on visitors. While the area covered by the plan is quite small – an alternative, rather than a challenge to the traditional city – it was an early and influential example of a new start in urban design.

Stein took his ideas further with two developments beyond the city boundary: Radburn in New Jersey in 1928 and Chatham Village outside Pittsburg in 1931. Both consist of single-family houses set on large garden lots, both are designed to accommodate the automobile. While the eighty-six-acre Chatham Village was a financial success, Radburn was only five months into construction when the 1929 stock-market crash occurred and the development was soon abandoned after only 677 units were completed. However, the development outlined an approach to houses on cul-de-sacs, removed from the bustle of a city – a hallmark of modern residential design. Humphrey Carver, Canada's influential planner, said, 'Radburn is a landmark in man's quest for a better way of living ... a noble fragment ... an entirely new way of living at peace with the automobile' (Carver 1975, 39–40). The cul-de-sacs are for cars; the extensive footpaths for people.

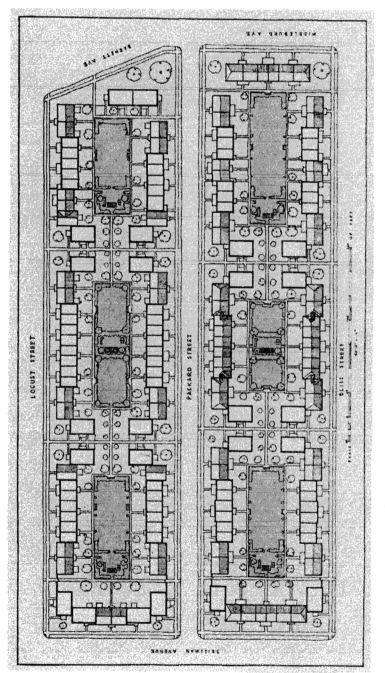

Sunnyside Gardens, New York. Clarence Stein and Henry Wright, 1924. This plan might be seen as a modest Regent's Park, with the central park now become a small common interior yard and the houses attached together. Walkways lead not through a parklike setting, but along the edges of private yards. It unwittingly became the model for many townhouse condominium projects in the last quarter of the century. Stein 1951, 25

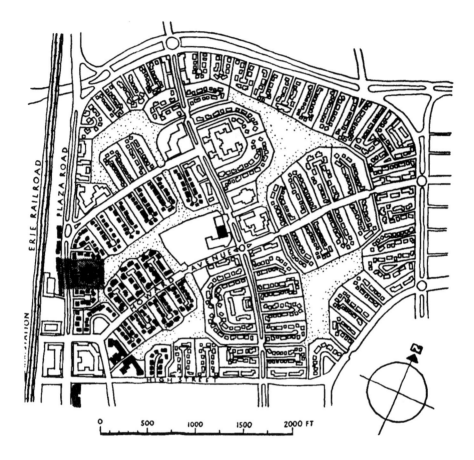

Radburn, New Jersey. Clarence Stein and Henry Wright, 1928. The site is broken into separate detached streets, each of which is surrounded by its own green space providing a sense of exclusivity. Stein 1951

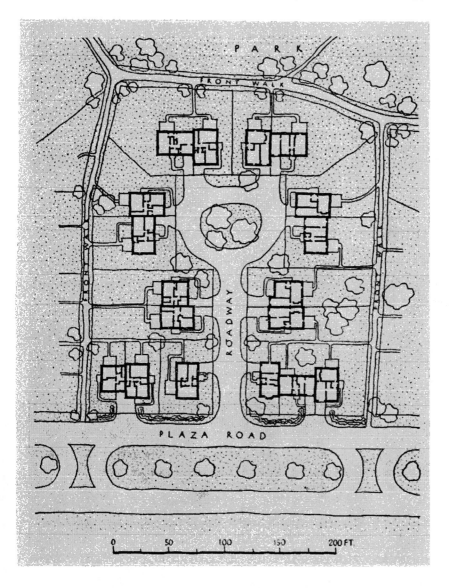

Radburn, detail. Each street is a cul-de-sac of a dozen homes. These isolated
elements are linked together by walkways. Stein 1951

Stein's most fully realized plan was for the eighty-acre Baldwin
Hills Village, now in the midst of Los Angeles, in 1941. It follows the Sunnyside/Garden City model, with blocks of homes
set among gardens and courtyards, carefully planned to contrast
with and be distinguishable from the urban fabric that sur-
rounds it. It illustrates his concern with achieving an appropriate population density. He felt the existing city was too dense,
echoing Howard and Wright: 'The great city, as a place to live
and work in, breaks down miserably ... it is perpetually breaking
down, and ... it will continue to do so as long as the pressure of
population within a limited area remains' (Lees 1985, 292).

Stein also looked for the best way to avoid the anonymous
quality of the city, and, with other planners, particularly his
colleague Henry Wright and Clarence Perry, he strongly advocated the idea that the neighbourhood unit was the basic
building block of cities. The centre of the neighbourhood
would be the school, surrounded by housing and community
services such as shops and institutions. Everything would be
within easy walking distance, this itself providing a limitation
on appropriate densities. These ideas would find full flower
thirty years later, with the building of Don Mills in Toronto in
the 1950s.

With the Depression of the 1930s and the Second World War,
there were few opportunities in the first half of the century to
put the new urban ideas further to the test. But one set of
proposals deserves mention – greenbelt towns – which might
be considered the culmination of the Howard and Wright kind
of thinking between the wars.

Greenbelt in Maryland is a cluster of Garden City structures
in a rural setting, almost coy in its attempt to evoke an organic
and 'natural' form. The towns of Greenhills, Greenbrook, and
Greendale are in the same style, and the names convey well
the major accomplishment, a drowning of the urban experience
in a sea of trees, shrubs, and grass. For all the straining by
their creators, these plans were hardly the challenges to traditional urban form called for by Howard and Wright. They
were interesting experiments, urban additions that showed the
kinds of opportunities available in designing suburban spaces,

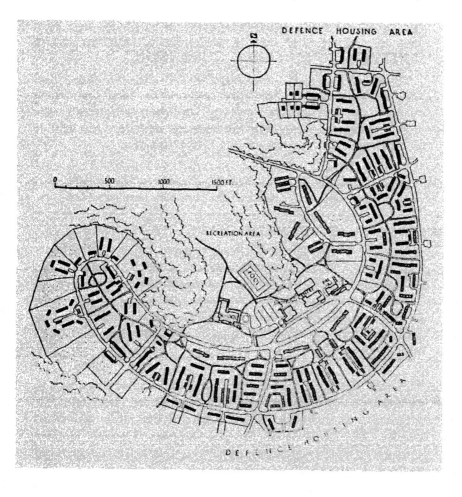

Greenhills, Ohio, 1938. The design feels very forced as the main road mean-
ders in fish-hook style. The rows of houses (loosed from the grid system of
Sunnyside Gardens) hug its edges like spokes, finding neither a place in the
country nor a place in the city. Stein 1951, 179

but hardly the New Jerusalems that had been prophesied. That kind of development awaited the explosion of urban growth that followed the end of the Second World War.

Although originally formulated in Europe, the ideas about the need for a new city found expression mostly in North America. In Europe, examples of suburban solutions in the vein of Olmsted and Stein are difficult to find. One author suggests an economic reason for this difference:

Despite the general lack of planning and other formal land-use controls, Europe's cities expanded more continuously and with higher densities at the leading edge than their North American counterparts ... it is clear that Europe was marked by higher opportunity costs for the agricultural land being lost, coupled with greater construction costs for brick and masonry compared with American lumber. Since the rich stood their central ground, the European urban periphery was settled by poorer people, on the average, again leading to higher density. One consequence today is that planners find nearby open space in European cities. (Hohenberg and Lees 1985, 307)

In North America it was a different world. There, according to Mumford, everyone was making proposals for yesterday's city of tomorrow. It was to these planners that Stein issued his clarion call at midcentury for new attempts to replace the old with the new. The explosion of urban growth that followed the Second World War seemed a perfect incubator for the ideas that had been around for half a century but that had yet to find widespread expression. Stein's hope that the ideal of the modern suburb would be realized came to pass – but first in Canada, not in the America to which his book was addressed.

2

City Building
in the
Modern Style

The new ideas in planning did not go unnoticed in Canada. Clarence Stein's clarion call to destroy the old and build the new had been published in full in the Canadian journal, *Community Planning Review*, in 1952, with admiring comment from Humphrey Carver, Canada's leading planning theoretician.

But the influence of the new thought had already been felt. New communities emerged on the edge of Canadian cities during the Great War, then in the developing resource towns after that war had ended. As the Second World War drew to a close, there was a significant outpouring of thought and energy, resulting in new large projects both in the hearts of cities and at their margins. By mid century in Toronto the tradition of the new was firmly established.

The plan for Lawrence Park in Toronto, prepared by Walter S. Brook in 1909, is an early example of the vibrancy of the new ideas. The traditional grid has been modified slightly, and open space is provided along a nearby stream, which in less adventurous schemes would simply have been contained in a sewer. The diagonal or sensually curving street is yet to be introduced.

By the time of the First World War, the ideas of Howard and the City Beautiful movement (as already noted in Lindenlea and Hydrostone) began to have expression in plans for Canadian resource towns. In the nineteenth century, plans developed by the Canadian Pacific Railway were carefully prepared, as company surveyors attempted to ensure maximum land values. Towns developed for mining or forest-product companies fared less well: formal corporate elements were often overwhelmed by squatters and those looking for work opportunities.

One author cites several reasons for the move to 'holistic planning': serious fires in the northern Ontario towns of Cobalt, Porcupine, Cochrane, and Matheson; the realization that these new settlements were likely to have more than just a temporary existence; typhoid epidemics and the wish to control communicable diseases; and the recognition by companies that a well-planned community proved an attraction to qualified labour (Artibise and Stetler 1986, 234–5).

The Iroquois Falls townsite, developed in 1915 by the Abitibi Power and Paper Company, is a fine example of the Garden

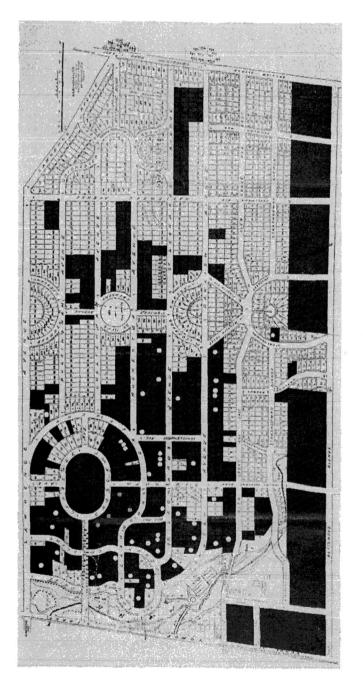

Lawrence Park, Toronto. Walter Brook, planner. The break with the traditional grid is tentative indeed. Curves seem to be interruptions rather than a new and pleasing element. It certainly is not a Riverside kind of community where city style has given way to countryside relaxation. Archives of Ontario

City approach finding physical form in Ontario. Saarinen notes the modified grid street pattern was used 'to provide a more graceful appearance.' Moreover, 'the link to the British tradition was given reinforcement through the use of street names such as Argyle, Buckingham, Cambridge, Devonshire, Essex, and Fyfe' (Artibise and Stelter 1986, 236). The overall arrangement was designed so that children would not have to pass through the business district on their way to school. Considerable thought was given to the maintenance of a rural atmosphere and the provision of open space. A main feature in this regard was the introduction of a combined educational and park complex containing sports facilities, recreational parks, and children's gardens. The intention was clearly to give the townsite a 'village green' and 'cottage' appearance.

Kapuskasing followed in 1921. The physical form is more distinguished, making a complete break with the grid system and reflecting with clarity the design precepts of Ebenezer Howard. There are two important distinctions from Iroquois Falls: the planning of Kapuskasing was under the direct control of government officials (indeed Premier E.C. Drury took a personal interest in the matter); and there was an attempt to create some independence for the town rather than leaving it entirely under the ownership and control of the Spruce Falls Pulp and Paper Company, which would provide its economic raison d'etre. The curvilinear street pattern, the handsome lot sizes, the greenbelt edging the river, and the careful attempt to create pleasing vistas are notable. The form of larger buildings (such as the hotel and the residences for single men) seems to be taken from Letchworth, or any other English town spawned by the Garden City movement: large sloping roofs which, though shingled, have the feel of being thatched; small windows, signalling the modest means of the inhabitants; and the carefully arranged lawns and gardens.

Similar structures to those found in Kapuskasing were built in Toronto at the same period. The influence came through Dr Charles Hastings, Toronto's medical officer of health, whose broad definition of public health included good housing. He helped lead the city into building the Bain Avenue Apartments

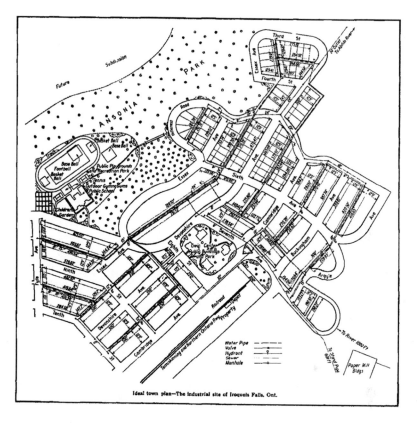

Ideal town plan—The industrial site of Iroquois Falls, Ont.

Iroquois Falls, Ontario, 1915. The grid plan has been modified to include curves, and the roads have been given English names, perhaps in homage to Ebenezer Howard. *Power and Place,* 236

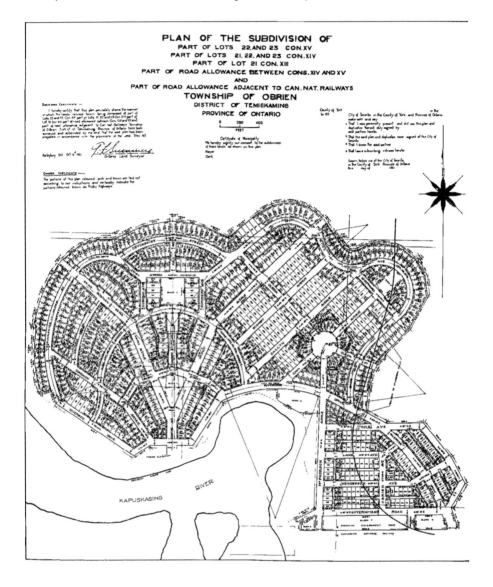

Kapuskasing, Ontario. J.A. Ellisa and A.V. Hall, 1922. The fan-shaped road pattern of Howard's Garden City is clearly evident, and the building forms differ little from those in Letchworth. *Power and Place*, 240

The Spruce Court Apartments in Toronto were begun in 1913, with a
second section built a decade later. The style derives from Letchworth,
with courtyards, fake half-timber decoration, and large sloping roofs.
Charlotte Sykes

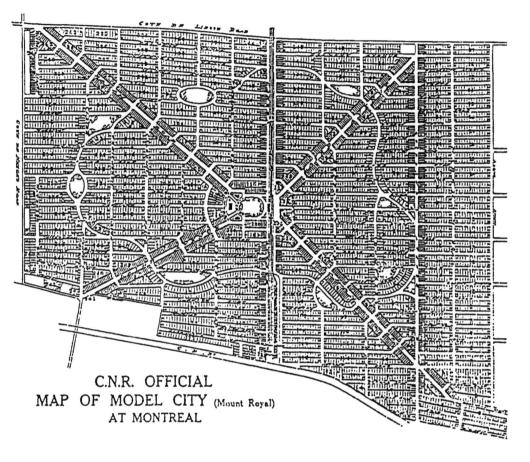

C.N.R. OFFICIAL
MAP OF MODEL CITY (Mount Royal)
AT MONTREAL

Mount Royal, Montreal. Frederick Todd, planner. Like Lawrence Park, the
road system seems not fully integrated: the curves interrupt the grid, as do
the diagonals, but seem an add-on or an after-thought.

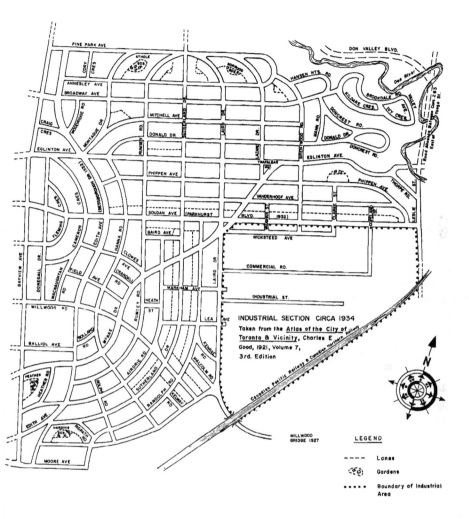

Leaside, Toronto. Frederick Todd, 1918? The plan is a modified, wavy grid, with a diagonal hangover from the City Beautiful movement thrown in.
Metro Toronto Reference Library

and the Spruce Court Apartments in the second decade of the century. Both projects were designed by A.S. Mathers and show the influence of Letchworth, including a similar courtyard arrangement around which units are set, and the same mimicking of roof, window, and garden design as in Kapuskasing.

In Montreal, new planning ideas were pursued in the 1910 plan for the Town of Mount Royal by Frederick Todd for the Canadian National Railway. The gently curving streets, the large lots, the sprinkling of neighbourhood parks, and the exclusion of nonresidential uses all show the City Beautiful influence. The house forms are more traditional, reflecting middle-class aspirations of the day, and without the strong design characteristics established by Ebenezer Howard.

Todd's next project – also for the CPR – was the design of the Town of Leaside after the site's purchase by the railway in 1912. The 1025 acres were incorporated as a town in 1913 after annexation with neighbouring East York failed. The York Land Company, which bought from the railway, was unable to raise money for servicing, and the development proceeded in a piecemeal fashion throughout the 1920s. It was only during the Depression years of the 1930s that development occurred on a consistent basis. The plan possesses a certain elegance. A diagonal road slices the site and is the location for nonresidential uses including administrative buildings, offices, and shops. Residential streets are set on a nicely modified grid, with boulevards between the roadway and the sidewalk. There must have been substantial tree planting: in the early 1990s, Leaside is a wonderfully leafy experience.

Leaside was one of the few developments in Canada to proceed during the Depression. During the Second World War, resources were devoted to military matters and it was not until the end of 1945 that new development again began to manifest itself.

The next distinct plan for a single industry town was Terrace Bay, in 1946, for the Kimberly-Clarke Pulp and Paper Company. The pulp plant was several miles away, permitting this town to be a residential enclave. Residences are protected from the main highway slicing through the site, and almost every street

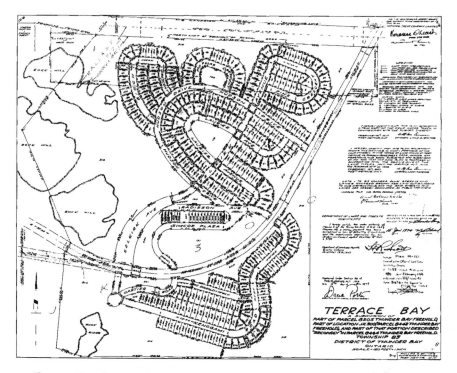

Terrace Bay, Ontario. Eugene Faludi, 1946. The streets are curvy and, unlike Iroquois Falls, where English references predominated, here we have roads named Selkirk, Laurier, Simcoe, as well as Pine, Birch, and Poplar. *Power and Place*, 247

Eugene Faludi explains his master plan of Toronto in 1943. Comay Planning Consultants Ltd. 1973, 40

doubles back on itself, creating a closed and protected community. The planner insisted that mature trees not be disturbed during construction, ensuring that country and city are firmly integrated. In keeping with ideas of creating a complete, harmonious community, the planner designed for income integration: 'An attempt was made to vary the style of the dwelling units on the basis of family composition and architectural variety rather than on the basis of occupational status' (Artibise and Stetler 1986, 248). Contrary to common understanding, new planning ideas were not a subtle attempt to separate income groups: more often, planners make explicit reference to their ideal of mixing incomes and family size.

The planner of Terrace Bay was Eugene Faludi, one of the earliest and most effective advocates of new planning. He was born in Budapest in 1897 and attended the architecture school of the University of Rome, where he obtained a doctorate in 1929. He established an architectural practice in Milan, and designed Italy's pavilion for the World Fair in Brussels in 1935. He fled fascist Italy in 1939 and, after spending a year in England, came to Canada in 1940. He began lecturing at both the University of Toronto and McGill University, and was retained by the city of Toronto, where he made a concerted effort to get the city interested in a thirty-year master plan even though the idea of general plans didn't become a favoured procedure for another twenty-five years. In 1944 he established Town Planning Consultants Limited with Anthony Adamson, and attracted a wide clientele of municipalities anxious to improve their physical presence: Regina, Hamilton, Windsor, Peterborough, Stratford, and Etobicoke, as well as Terrace Bay.

One common thread running through Faludi's planning commentary on the communities he studied is blight and decay. He suggested that more than one-quarter of Hamilton's residential areas was blighted; and more than one-seventh of Windsor's residential areas suffered the same fate. In most cases he found residential densities too high. He castigated Regina, noting there were '69 people or 17 families on one acre of land. This compares with the contemporary ideal of 6 to 8 families per acre' (Faludi 1946, 277). His strong advocacy of the new refrain, 'lower densities are better,' is apparent. He also began to attack the grid plan for roads, arguing that Regina's problem was that 'most of the residential areas have a gridiron street pattern which encourages through traffic' (Faludi 1946, 277).

Lecture notes from his classes at the University of Toronto in 1942 espouse Clarence Stein's notion that the neighbourhood is the basic building block of cities: 'In the older cities, most of the neighbourhoods have been absorbed by the growing mass of the city and have consequently lost their physical identities. In the modern conception of planning, the first goal is to re-establish those characteristics that will make the decaying and vanishing neighbourhoods a flourishing organism again.' (Faludi 1944)

Anthony Adamson was a fellow teacher at the University of Toronto. Born in Canada early in the century, he had been educated in England but returned to Toronto to form an architectural partnership with Eric Arthur in 1929. With Arthur, Adamson worked on the report of the lieutenant-governor of Ontario, H.A. Bruce, on Toronto housing conditions early in the Depression. The report documented in painful detail the poverty and poor housing conditions that existed in downtown Toronto, and is now generally seen as the progenitor of the movement that pushed successfully two decades later for a major urban renewal and public housing program.

Adamson remembers the Bruce report as 'a concoction of current thinking of the time,' and in it he provided a prescient sketch of a superblock redevelopment proposal for an inner-city neighbourhood (see Regent Park North, 71ff). But Adamson was forced to leave the city because of illness in 1935, and he did not return until 1943. The City of Toronto Planning Board had been established the previous year, and Adamson returned just in time for the release of the board's ambitious master plan for Toronto. Faludi, the city's consultant, was the major force behind this plan.

The master plan dealt mostly with the bigger issues, such as distribution of employment and residential areas, roads and transit, and green belts. But it also contained hints of the

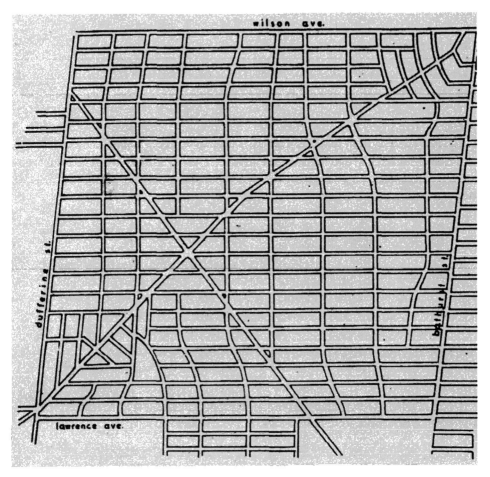

Dufferin/Lawrence subdivisions, Toronto. Eugene Faludi, 1943. Above is
the 'traditional' plan of subdivision: on the right, Faludi's proposed improvement, stressing irregularity, a hierarchy of public thoroughfares, a seg-
regation of different housing types, and 'more open planning' (according to
the caption) because of the 'need of every neighbourhood for open space in
order to make itself perpetuating.' Adamson and Faludi 1944

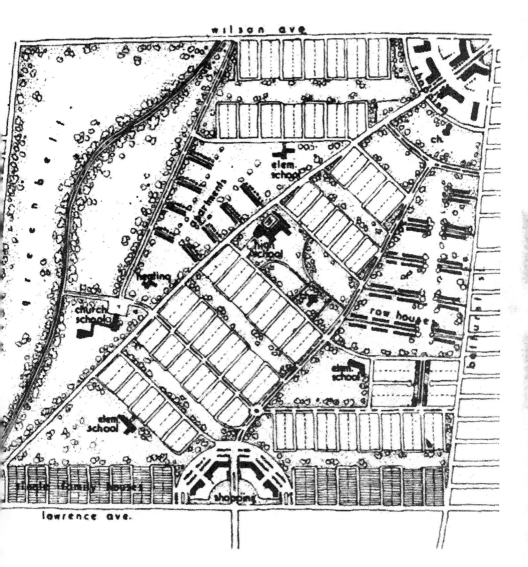

direction that should be pursued in the redesign of individual neighbourhoods. One sketch showed the kinds of changes that should be made to a downtown neighbourhood, generally demolishing it and starting again. Another sketch showed what might be done on the outskirts of the city as an alternative to a regular grid layout of streets. Both sketches are imaginary. But as the master plan notes, the exercise 'contrasts existing methods of subdivision for residential building within the possibilities of a planned neighbourhood of the same area. It is self-explanatory and graphically shows the policy of the [Planning] Board towards more open planning, the reasons for the necessity of which it states as the need of every neighbourhood for open space in order to make it self perpetuating' (Adamson and Faludi 1944, 128).

The first sketch shows a grid system broken by diagonals, as might be expected in the normal course of events. This layout would provide for traditional single family houses ranged along streets, perhaps broken by several commercial structures on arterials. The second is more complicated. Various housing forms are included, with discrete locations provided for schools, churches, and a district heating plant. Much of the site is left as greenbelt, and the road system is generally discontinuous. Some buildings do not face directly onto roads but are surrounded by green space. Faludi was to follow this trend in the plans he developed over the next few years.

The plan also commented on what should happen to the existing city:

If demolition of worn-out buildings is to be permitted to take its normal course, which is a hit or miss affair with here and there the appearance of vacant lands, the process of haphazard rebuilding will never recreate a brand new development over any sizable area. The progress of blight will no doubt be retarded but the sources of the disease will remain to infect not only these areas, but the surrounding areas as well...

Certainly every effort should be made in rebuilding the older residential areas, to create such conditions of plan and to provide such permanent amenities as will create a residential character of

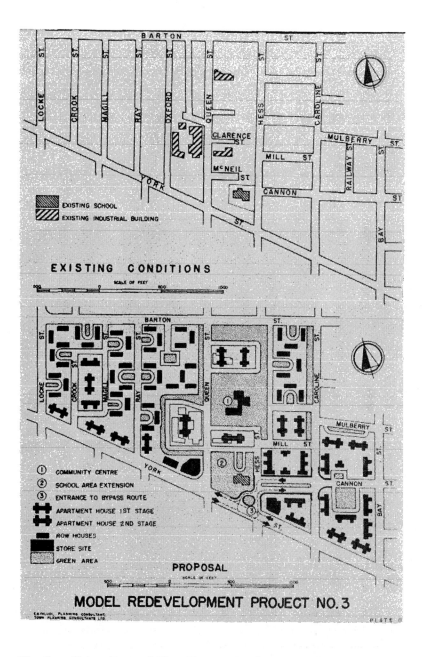

Hamilton Urban Renewal Plan. Eugene Faludi, 1943. Faludi's plan breaks
up the road system and replaces single-family houses with the same blocks of
housing structures found in Stein's plans for Sunnyside or Baldwin Village.
Faludi Papers, Metropolitan Toronto Reference Library

the most modern type quite the equal of, if not superior to that pertaining in the newest suburban areas. (Adamson and Faludi 1944, 128)

The plan went on to discuss clearance of a large area to the east of downtown, later to be called Regent Park.

Adamson remembered that he was 'mesmerized by Radburn,' and that everyone's thinking was dominated by the new planning ideas: the greenbelt, the satellite town, the neighbourhood unit, the superblock. 'I thought something was needed in the way of a profession,' he recalled, and 'I said, let's form a service to make planning more available' (Adamsom interview, July 1989). When Adamson formed Town Planning Consultants Limited with Faludi; he saw the new firm as a service organization:'There was no money in it. If there was money, then Faludi did it.' The company, Adamson claimed, began to grind out official plans under the new Planning Act passed by Ontario at the end of the war. Adamson became more involved in restoration architecture, and left the planning work to Faludi and others.

In 1947 Faludi released his master plan for Hamilton. The plan permitted him to tie together thoughts about urban decay, the road system, and the neighbourhood in a much more intimate way than was possible in the Toronto plan: 'Decline has been spreading progressively for years. In order to provide decent living conditions and to stop the spread of further deterioration all over the city, the redevelopment of such blighted areas is imperative ... Rehabilitation can be accomplished only by the wholesale attack on the problem involving replanning and rebuilding on a large scale' (Faludi 1947, 50). As the diagram shows, Faludi's solution is one urged on many Canadian cities over the next few decades: clear away the old, close streets, and build residential structures with no clear relationship to city streets. It was a formula that urban renewal planners, persuaded by the idea of urban decay, would use many times over.

A spectacular example of Faludi's vision of the new city is Thorncrest Village, now in the midst of suburban Etobicoke.

When it was purchased by developer Marshall Foss in the early 1940s it was just a farmer's field several miles west of the developed urban area.

Thorncrest is a hundred-acre site, bounded by arterials Islington Avenue, Rathburn Road, and Kipling Avenue, and residential development to the north. The guiding idea behind the plan is the greenbelt town. Faludi twisted a lazy road across the site, and from it branched off cul-de-sacs. A small shopping plaza was created at the southeast corner of the site, and in the centre of the development are tennis courts and a recreation centre operated as a private club for Thorncrest residents. Sprinkled across the site are 180 houses, sited to take full advantage of topography and natural light. Lots are generally half an acre, large enough to accommodate septic tanks since the community was a considerable distance from the city's sewer system. The houses were in a style new to Toronto: generally single storey, broadside to the street, sitting on a concrete slab rather than on a basement. While Faludi did not design each home, he ensured there were building controls. Since the site was owned by a single company – it was unusual at this time to find development by one company occurring in such large parcels – the owner could select the individual buyers and ensure they would arrange for competent builders. The developer reserved the right to approve house designs and materials used, and clearly he exercised considerable influence since the homes seem cut from the same cloth.

The approach was not to everyone's liking. As Faludi wrote in 1950:

Thorncrest Village in the spring of 1946 looked too radical to make it acceptable to realters, mortgage investors, municipal engineers, councillors and the 'common man' for whom a brave new world was supposed to be built. All of them, in their own way, were right to some extent. It was a new environment in which at first glance, there appeared to be too many uncertainties and imponderables.

The realter was against the basementless house with large picture windows and radiant floor heating. It's use and economy during the long Canadian winter had to be proved first.

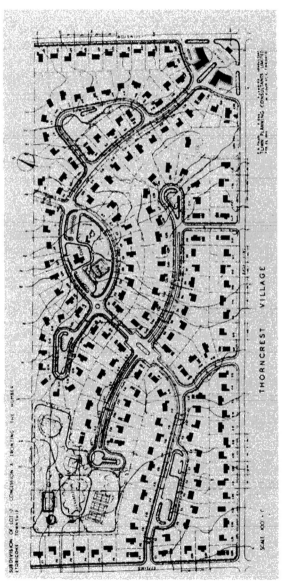

Thorncrest Village, Toronto. Eugene Faludi, 1945. The curves of the roadways have a languid feel about them, appropriate to create a quiet country feeling on the edge of a growing city. Toronto Real Estate Board

The mortgage investor was doubtful whether the maintenance and operating costs of the public services could be kept up at least at the same rate as in traditionally built communities.

The municipal engineer complained that curved roads represented 20–40 per cent higher cost in watermains and hydro installations; that cul-de-sacs, in addition to higher installation costs for public utilities, were difficult to clean with standard snowploughs.

For the municipal councillor, 'anybody who would live in such an unusual place must be socially and morally unstable' and therefore not desirable in the municipality.

The 'common man,' for whom we intended this community, was against everything. He disapproved the design of the houses in general. He disliked the free placement in relation to lot lines and neighbouring houses. He utterly rejected the idea of the living room being oriented towards the south and not towards the street. He did not believe that curved streets would slow down the speed of cars; on the contrary, curved roads represented to him a driving and parking nuisance. He was also afraid of the operating cost of the swimming pool and community hall and the social life connected with it. (Faludi 1950, 77)

There's little question but that Faludi was overstating the case, particularly since the homes sold well. But he was writing for a planning audience that would share his frustration with objectors to the new ideas, an audience that would be sympathetic to his aspirations. He went on: 'Nevertheless, there were people who liked the idea of this novel setting. They were the people who always support progress and advanced thoughts.'

An appeal to the new, to progress, has been the last resort of many twentieth-century planners and artists in the face of hostile criticism. As we shall see, the idea that a planning idea should be accepted simply because it was new and different, and not because it had any intrinsic merit, is one that would gain ground. Faludi claimed that a majority of those who purchased homes in Thorncrest Village 'are employed in publicity, advertising and radio, which depends in pioneering in thought.'

As soon as Thorncrest was completed, Faludi was retained by Home Smith and Co, the most significant developer on

Toronto's western boundary, to design a 300-acre site across Islington Avenue from Thorncrest Village, stretching east to Royal York Road. He modified his ideas somewhat for this larger site, including some garden apartments among the single family homes on lots ranging from fifty-five to seventy-five feet frontage. The site was cut by a diagonal street (the same diagonal as in the sketch in Toronto's master plan?), off which emanated an number of cul-de-sacs and looping roads. There is a more formal air about Kingsway, as the area began to be called. The lot system is more regular, with fewer chances to achieve the best environmental siting for each house, and all roads have sidewalks rather than ditches. The central park contains not only recreational and social facilities but also a school. The garden apartments – a total of 500 units in buildings each containing about a dozen units – are clustered in three locations on the site. It is as though the Thorncrest ideas have been modified just enough to change the neighbourhood from being predominantly rural to predominantly urban. This community was called Humber Valley Village by Faludi, but is widely known as the Kingsway, after the diagonal street that sweeps across the tract.

Faludi was proud of his work, and drew some conclusions about what Canadians wanted in the way of new communities: 'Humber Valley Village means something more to planners. It verifies our belief that Canadians prefer to live close to nature and that they are not attracted by multi-storey warehouses with the most up-to-date facilities' (Faludi 1950, 141). Forty years later, Thorncrest Village and the Kingsway both continue to exert a presence, even though they are now completely surrounded by suburban development. In Thorncrest, the houses still feel as though they are luxuriant country cottages in harmony with their surroundings, and the roadway – still without sidewalks – is bounded by the appropriately soft edge of shallow ditches. It exudes an aura of exclusivity, of distinct homes set in a refined greenery that is a world apart to the traditional nineteenth-century city. Unfortunately, in the late 1980s, a number of homes were demolished and replaced with larger out-of-place monsters.

As Thorncrest Village and Humber Valley Village show, the

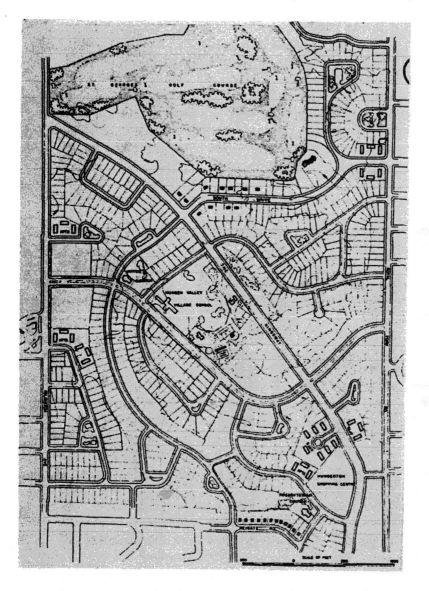

Humber Valley Village, Toronto. Eugene Faludi, 1949. The larger site has
resulted in a more modest plan – although the curved roads have more
sweep – than Thorncrest Village, and nothing like the innovation attempted
in the 1943 plan for the Dufferin/Lawrence intersection. Toronto Real
Estate Board

end of the Second World War proved the turning point for development opportunities – and for the planning thinking that had been bubbling for half a century. Intellectuals embraced the new approaches and attempted to have them implemented. In Ontario, the major challenge – now that the war had ended – was to address problems of decayed housing in the existing city. The way to do that was with new plans.

Since the early 1930s slum clearance and public housing had been gaining powerful support in American cities. The first public housing project in that country was built in Cleveland in the early 1930s. At the same time, these concerns found focus in Toronto in a luncheon speech by Lieutenant-Governor Herbert Bruce. The ensuing Bruce report detailed slum conditions in Toronto and suggested that most of the city's downtown residential areas – everything south of College/Carlton streets, from Dovercourt on the west to the Don River on the east – should be torn down, and a fresh start made. The report argued:

It seems the only availing remedy in Toronto is planned decentralization which will take the outmoded factory away from our congested central areas and substitute for it in the outskirts a modern building. That would permit workers to establish their homes convenient to their work in surroundings where their children would learn by experience that grass is a green living and loving carpet and that there are really and truly other and lovelier flowers than those of the lithographed calender that hangs on the cracked, crumbling, and soiled wall of a murky room into which the suns rays have never penetrated. It seems to me also that as we evacuate those factories and hovels, we must raze them and bury the distressing memory of them in fine central parks and recreation centres. (Committee to Enquire into Housing Conditions, 1934)

The quotation bears remarkable similarities to Ebenezer Howard's great claim: 'I will undertake, then, to show how in "town-country" equal, nay better, opportunities of social intercourse may be enjoyed than are enjoyed in any crowded city, while yet the beauties of nature may encompass and enfold

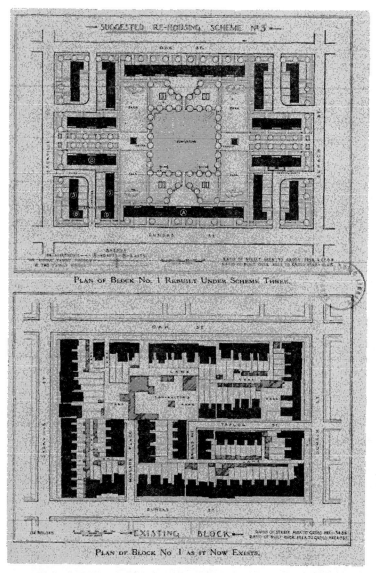

PLAN OF BLOCK No. 1 REBUILT UNDER SCHEME THREE.

PLAN OF BLOCK No. 1 AS IT NOW EXISTS.

Regent Park North, Toronto. Bruce Report, 1932. These sketches were prepared by Eric Arthur and A.A. Adamson, and the suggested scheme shows all the characteristics of modernism – a rejection of the old, its replacement with something alien, and a desire to relegate housing to the edges in order to maximize common open space. Metropolitan Toronto Reference Library

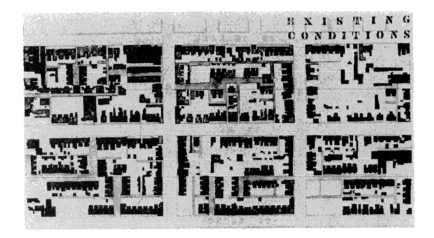

Regent Park North, Toronto. Six blocks with laneways and a mix of residential, commercial, and industrial uses, as existing in the 1930s. Adamson and Faludi 1944

Regent Park North, Toronto. Eugene Faludi, 1943. Faludi's contribution to replanning the superblock is a diagonal road, an element that seems to dominate most designs in the 1943 master plan for Toronto. Adamson and Faludi 1944

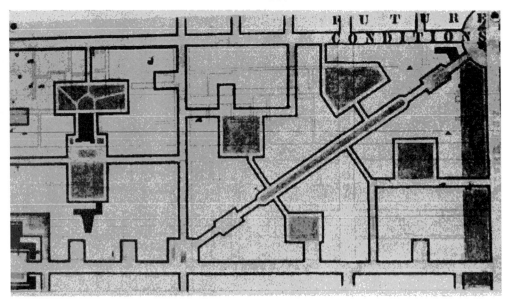

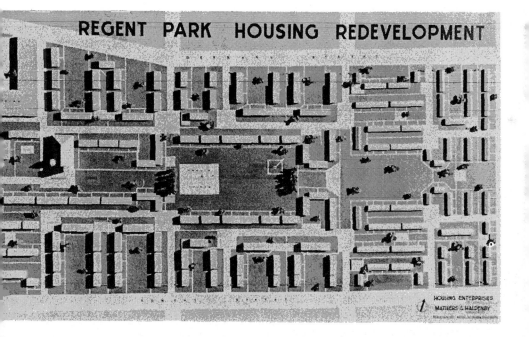

Regent Park North, Toronto. Mathers and Haldenby, 1946. The plan is little more than an expansion on that found in the Bruce report. Metropolitan Toronto Reference Library

each dweller therein' (Howard 1965, 48). The Bruce report endorses Stein's Radburn plan and suggests several different approaches for a superblock replacing some of the worst of the city's housing. The sketches were prepared by Anthony Adamson and Eric Arthur.

All plans called for the demolition of existing row housing and factories and the construction of two- or three-storey apartment structures on the periphery of the site, leaving the central space open for a large green park. Existing buildings covered about a third of the land area; after development, that figure would be cut in half, to 17 per cent. The Bruce report implicitly endorsed the idea that lower densities – or at least an increase in green space and a feeling that densities were lower – were better.

The plans in the Bruce report were followed by Faludi's own ideas for the site in the 1943 master plan for the city: the diagonal street is in evidence (it is to be largely a pedestrian way, with parking at either end), and 72 per cent of the land is to be open space. About 80 per cent of the housing units are to be in three-storey structures (Adamson and Faludi 1944, 128).

As the war drew to an end, there was an unleashing of energies and ideas about planning and building that had been pent up since the later 1920s. In 1944 the federal government passed the National Housing Act (NHA), more formally entitled 'An Act to promote the construction of new houses and the repair and maintenance of existing houses and improvement of housing and living standards and the expansion of employment in the post-war period.' The same year the government's Advisory Committee on Reconstruction published its report, 'Housing and Community Planning.' Two years later Central Mortgage and Housing Corporation (CMHC), the federal government's agency for implementing housing policy, was established.

In 1946 the Ontario government passed its first comprehensive Planning Act, providing a framework for subdivisions and land investment. An earlier statute in 1937 had set down guidelines for some municipalities, but the 1944 act permitted official plans and general planning controls to be exercised by any municipality. At the same time, the Federal Insurance Act was amended to permit insurance companies to invest in land development, providing a very large source of new capital to help meet Canada's immense housing needs as soldiers returned home and the baby boom was about to begin.

In 1944 a group called the Citizens' Housing and Planning Association emerged. It was headed by social activists of the day, including Harold Clark, Albert Rose, and Humphrey Carver who were involved in teaching social work and related subjects at the University of Toronto, with the view to pushing for the construction of affordable housing. The association's immediate aim was to implement the Bruce report, and specifically to redevelop a forty-two-acre area in downtown east Toronto that had been defined in the report as one of the worst slum areas in the city. City planners had renewed interest in the site with a report published in 1944 which proposed construction similar to that in the Bruce report, increasing population from 3700 to 4400 and play space from nil to almost eight acres. The redevelopment plan included in the 1944 report is at considerable variance to that found in the Bruce report, save for the basic premise – that there should be total demolition and a new start.

The association agitated for action and convinced city council to place the following question on the ballot in the January 1947 election:

Are you in favour of the city undertaking as a low cost or moderate cost rental housing project, with possible government assistance, the clearing, replanning, rehabilitation and modernization of the area bounded by Parliament, River, Gerrard and Dundas Streets known as Regent Park North, at an estimated cost of $5,900,000? (Rose 1958, 65)

The voters supported the resolution, 30,000 to 18,000 votes. Where the name Regent Park came from is unclear, but in all probability it is derived from John Nash's 1812 plan for London, Regent's Park, where large elegant mansions were placed in a park-like setting. The irony could hardly be more clear.

There seemed to be little debate about what a new plan for this area should be like: it was as though the matter had been settled by the Bruce report, the 1943 master plan, and the subsequent report from city planners. A plan was prepared – apparently on speculation – by the architectural firm of Mathers and Haldenby in 1946 for Housing Enterprises Limited, a limited dividend company established by Canadian insurance companies under the NHA of 1944. According to Adamson, the proponents of Regent Park feared the larger firms and opted for a relatively unknown architect, J.E. Hoare, who might be expected to be less expensive. It was his plan that was finally used.

Hoare's plan bears a striking resemblance to Faludi's ideas for improving Hamilton in 1942 and to the Cedar Heights public housing project built in Cleveland in 1934. In each case, a cruciform building shape – reminiscent of Le Corbusier – is dominant. All plans feature a surfeit of open space surrounding the buildings. The site is kept free from roads, and the urban fabric has been totally destroyed and replaced.

There are a few row houses, but most homes are located in apartment structures varying in height from three to six stories. All buildings are done in red brick and have a monotonous look and feel, products of the same cookie cutter. Buildings float in a sea of grass, and are placed on the site with little reference to roads.

An administrative centre and recreational complex were included in the plan, as was a church near the western edge of the site, replacing several churches to be demolished. No retail facilities were included. The location of the recreation building makes it clear it is for project residents only, not for the wider community.

As the National Film Board film *Farewell to Oak Street* showed, displaced tenants were pleased with the results. In place of a home in often deplorable condition at a rent that took a large portion of the family income, they were moved into a large new apartment with rent based on income. The Regent Park experiment was not simply a matter of new planning: it was also social reform. But the social reform was based on the idea

Regent Park North, Toronto. J.E. Hoare, 1947. This plan follows the precepts of building form laid out by Faludi in his plan for Hamilton earlier this decade – cruciform buildings, from the American public housing tradition – rather than the housing slabs of Mathers and Haldenby or Faludi. This plan comes closest to reflecting what was actually built, although the monotony of three-storey structures was lightened by the introduction of several six-storey buildings. Rose 1958

that the old city had to be replaced, not simply modified.

A 1951 booklet published by the Housing Authority of Toronto (which managed the project) summarized the basic approach taken, one that replicates the ideas of Clarence Stein:

Merely to permit the building of new residential buildings on the existing street pattern, and as a patchwork program applied to the present situation, is to fail to create the attractive surroundings which are essential. Reconstruction must, therefore, consist in the clearing out of the existing buildings, the redesign of the street plan to eliminate through traffic and to provide adequate amenities in the form of parks and children's playgrounds, and the rebuilding of the whole area. (Housing Authority of Toronto 1951, 1–2)

Regent Park North proved to be the start of a new way of redesigning existing urban space in Canada. Social reform and land-use planning began to seem inseparable, and those who advocated social reform could be expected, as Ebenezer Howard had done in 1898, to plump for new planning approaches. Humphrey Carver, who was interested in addressing the housing crisis immediately after the war, recognized the importance that planning would play in achieving this goal. In 1948 he published *Housing for Canadians* and pointed to the need for of planning in achieving affordable housing:

In planning the construction of new communities it is necessary not only to lay out sites but also to determine the sequence of operations. In this sense community planning is similar to the planning of any other kind of industrial process; it may be compared with the designing of the process by which the component parts of automobiles are delivered to the assembly line in a rational sequence so that the finished products can be brought to completion as economically and rapidly as possible. (Carver 1948, 34)

In 1950 the Toronto Real Estate Board trumpeted the new kind of city building with publication of a small booklet (Faludi 1952). As editor, Faludi was given the opportunity to publish the plans and sketches of new projects. Several new subdivisions

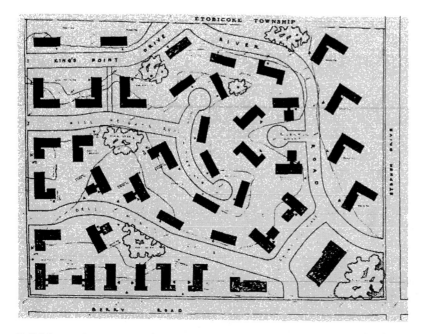

Bell Manor, Etobicoke, 1949. Note the apparent random placement of apartment buildings, which vary in height from three to five storeys. Toronto Real Estate Board

Shopping centre. Faludi, 1951. The sketch captures the sense of limitless space planners felt they had at their disposal now the automobile was available to most families. Toronto Real Estate Board

were shown, including the Kingsway, and the newest invention
fresh from the United States – shopping centres. The Bell
Manor apartment complex was one of the most radical plans
in this collection. It consists of several dozen small apartment
buildings scattered almost at random over a field: it was the
one clear example in the booklet of a plan that attempted to
sever any relationship between the building and the street.
The idea of experimentation in Bell Manor may well have
emerged from the same instructions given to British planners
for the new town of Peterlee a few years later: 'Do what you
like but don't do what we have done before' (Edwards 1981,
229). Indeed, the planners did just that in Peterlee, tossing out
commonly held perceptions about how living space worked:
'We decided we would not tolerate the backgarden mania of
the new town with its chicken wire fences. We decided that
there would be no front and back in the normally accepted
way' (Edwards 1981, 231).

As the idea of alternative urban forms gained momentum,
so did the role of the planners. Faludi was not alone. Robert
Fishman puts it this way:

Between the old city and the new stands the planner. He sees beyond the social conflicts of his time to the true order of industrial
society. His imagination is the first to comprehend the common
good and give it form as a design for a new kind of community. This
is the source of his authority, an authority that Howard, Wright and
Le Corbusier believed to be deeper and truer than that of any
political leader. For the planner does not sponsor the goals of any
single group. Rather, he works to create a society in which all social
differences would be reconciled. (Fishman 1977, 266)

Similar sentiments were provoked by those replanning Ajax,
a community of 4000 residents on the eastern edge of Toronto
built to produce munitions for Canadian forces during the
Second World War. CMHC officials recognized their obligations
but also the remarkable opportunity:

The town planner is probably the most consistently frustrated
professional man. This is so because he is generally dealing with

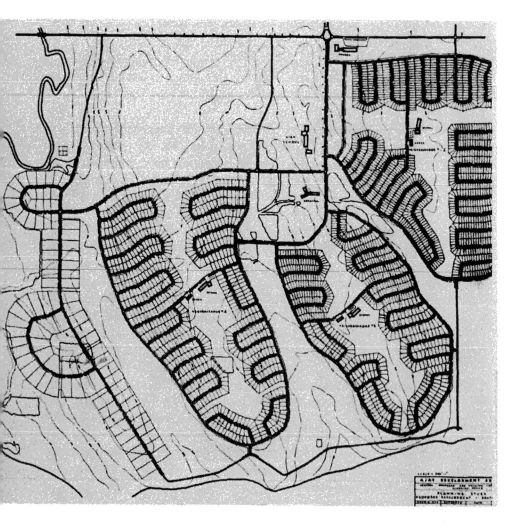

Ajax, Ontario. Barker, 1951. The change in thinking within the decade, from the curving streets of Thorncrest Village and Kingsway to the looping roads of Barker's neighbourhoods, is remarkable. It is as though Radburn had been rediscovered. Community Planning Review

existing cities, bedeviled with traffic congestion, obsolete housing, and all the familiar manifestations of modern civilization.

By comparison, Ajax presented a clean, uncomplicated, technical problem. We had no local politics with which to contend, and no municipal council to convince or pacify. (Barker 1951, 15)

Kent Barker, who was responsible for CMHC's planning work here, noted that 'space, pure and simple, is in abundant supply' (Barker 1951, 10) and he proposed four neighbourhoods of looping roads, each separated by green space so that 'no house ... will be more than 200 yards from a park or greenbelt' (Barker 1951, 14). One object of the plan was to separate uses 'on the theory that a mixture of dwellings and factories is equally undesirable, whether the district is designated residential or industrial'; another was to encourage experimentation with building forms: 'The design of multiple dwellings affords the architect opportunities for grouping the buildings in unconventional patterns. New ideas should not be ruled out merely because they were unforeseen and consequently may not conform to the letter of the law' (Barker 1951, 10).

The difference between the plan for Ajax and that used for the town built during the Second World War is quite evident. The latter is based on a modified grid road pattern, where the modification consists of slightly bending otherwise straight streets. The former is an entirely different and contrasting road configuration, protecting each community from intrusion rather than providing easy access to every part of the built-up city.

Ajax represented the latest planning thinking on how government could develop a new town, which was the way new communities were built in the United Kingdom. In Canada, however, the largest and most influential new communities were planned and built by the private sector. As private sector initiatives, Thorncrest and Humber Valley Village led the way for the largest and most influential corporate suburb in the country, Don Mills.

3

Don Mills:
Canada's First
Corporate
Suburb

Don Mills is the most influential development in Canada during the twentieth century. The style it established has become
so pervasive that many people assume it is the only way residential communities can be built. Moreover, the economic
arrangements underpinning Don Mills have been widely used
by developers who hope to repeat its staggering economic
success.

In 1947 E.P. Taylor, began to purchase farm land north and
east of Toronto. The area he chose was somewhat isolated
from the urban area that had developed since the 1830s: the site
was cut off from Toronto on the west, south, and east by
ravines through which ran railway lines leading to the heart of
the city, seven miles away.

Taylor was one of Canada's most successful corporate businessmen. His prime success had come from combining small
locally-based breweries into a single company that was far more
powerful and profitable than the parts of which it had been
made. The farm land was purchased through his company,
O'Keefe Realty Limited, a subsidiary of O'Keefe Breweries,
and many thought Taylor intended to construct a large new
plant surrounded by workers' housing.

Taylor had limited but influential experience in real estate.
Shortly after the Second World War, when he learned that a
development of smaller homes was in process close to his estate
on Bayview Avenue in Toronto, he intervened to buy the site
and subdivide it into larger lots for a development known as
Wrentham Estates. York Mills Plaza, one of the earliest Canadian
shopping plazas, was developed on the north-east corner of
Wrentham Estates. Financial arrangements for this development
were standard for the time: Taylor sold individual lots to small
builders for a very good price of $3200 a lot, the builders con-
structed a house and then sold the package, earning a profit,
they hoped, not only on the house but also on the land. Taylor
undoubtedly recognized there were ways to capture the increase
in land value, rather than see it flow into the pockets of the
builders, and thus realize even larger profits than those produced by this first land development venture.

By 1952 Taylor had purchased thirty-one parcels of land

totalling 2063 acres, but since 1950 it had been clear more was to be built than simply a brewery. Few people knew exactly what Taylor had in mind or what model he might follow. In Britain several new towns had been planned within five years of the end of the war, and in the United States there was considerable discussion about opportunities to do the same. The example of the privately sponsored Levittown on Long Island was criticized by planners: it was not a planned new town but simply an unending collection of streets lined by repetitious and inexpensive houses. In Canada, Humphrey Carver showed in his influential *Houses for Canadians* how a new community could be laid out, touting a private development rather than following the British approach with government as the sponsor. If Taylor's scheme was to proceed, it would be unprecedented on either side of the Atlantic.

The exact genesis of Taylor's new community idea is unclear. It may have come from John Layng, the architect who had laid out York Mills Plaza. He was credited by the 1953 press release issued by Don Mills Development Limited with the original plan. Or it may have come from Macklin Hancock, a student of landscape architecture who, through his father's company Cooksville Nursery, had devised landscape and planning ideas for both Wrentham Estates and York Mills Plaza. Hancock is mentioned in the same press release as the head of the firm's planning department.

In 1951 Taylor's company had enough ideas about the new community to call together members of the North York Council and present a proposal. A meeting was arranged at the prestigious Granite Club and a model of a residential development was shown. For its part, North York Council had hired none other than Eugene Faludi to review the plans: he suggested that industrial uses should be added to balance the assessment and tax loads. That suggestion was later incorporated into the scheme.

The same year, discussions were undertaken with officials from the Urban Land Institute, an American organization interested in development, and the scheme was presented to members in both Seattle and Cincinnati. Early in 1952, members of the institute visited the site and gave approval to the plans.

In late 1951 Taylor and Layng had an unexplained falling-out. At this time Hancock, who as the son-in-law of Carl Fraser, Taylor's executive assistant, had considerable informal influence, was attending town-planning classes at Harvard University, working towards a postgraduate degree. He was studying under such exponents of new town theory as Sir William Holford, Hadeo Sasaki, and Walter Gropius. Hancock was asked to take over as chief planner, but his Harvard teachers refused to give him credit for this work, arguing that a scheme of this magnitude would never come to fruition and that he would probably be back in class in a few months. Hancock decided to take the appointment anyway, and immediately hired several young Toronto architects to work with him: Douglas Lee, Henry Fliess, and James Murray. Hancock consulted Holford on the planning work, visiting him in England and later giving him a tour of the site when the plan received his official blessing. One unsubstantiated rumour has it that, at a dinner in England, Holford drew a plan on a napkin and that Hancock used this sketch as his basic model.

There were questions as to what to call the new community. Yorktown (mimicking Toronto's early name as a city) and Eptown (after E.P. himself) were early suggestions, but in 1952 Hancock suggested Don Mills – in the northeast corner of the site there was a mill on the Don River – and that name stuck.

Five concepts informed Hancock's remarkable plan: neighbourhoods, a discontinuous road system, a profusion of green space, new house forms and new lot configurations, and a separation of uses and activities.

The most important structural element was the neighbourhood. The land was neatly cut into four by the intersection of two roads, Lawrence Avenue and what is now called Don Mills Road, and each quadrant was treated as a separate neighbourhood. This use of the neighbourhood unit as a key building block of a residential plan had first been suggested by Clarence Perry in his work for the Regional Plan of New York in 1929, then expanded in his 1939 book, *Housing for the*

In 1953, before construction had begun in Don Mills, the intersection of Lawrence Avenue and Don Mills was a quiet rural corner. The information centre for the first homes in Don Mills is at centre left. Metropolitan Toronto Reference Library

Machine Age. The power of the idea is best caught by the American developer, William Rouse:

The fact is that the city is out of scale with the human being. It is beyond his scope and capacity. It is unmanageable. It is only in an abstract way that the human individual can feel a part of his city. We must make the city consist of communities which are in human scale – communities which the individual can feel part of and for the life of which he can feel a sense of participation and responsibility. This means a city of neighbourhoods. (McConnell 1959, 82)

The more cynical view of the neighbourhood idea was expressed by Lewis Mumford:

Clarence Perry had in effect restored, with modern ideas and modern facilities, above all with self-conscious art, one of the oldest components of the city, the quarter, which we found in early Mesopotamia. But he had transposed the temple or church as the attractive nucleus into the school and the community centre. (Mumford 1961, 501)

The neighbourhood idea had been much talked about since 1929. In *Houses for Canadians,* Carver saw the neighbourhood as the basic building block of planning: it was on the neighbourhood that one could hang all the necessary numbers to determine land use. Carver started with the least dense part of the city of Toronto, Lawrence Park, and then worked downward to something even less dense as the model neighbourhood:

The [City of Toronto] Planning Board was able to identify seventy-eight neighbourhoods within the city boundaries, varying in size from 150 to 330 acres with an average of about 250 acres. In the older parts of the city there were found to be from 60 to 100 persons per acre – or a population of about 20,000 in a 250 acre neighbourhood. In the more modern part of the city that lies north of the Canadian Pacific Railway line there were found to be from 30 to 60 persons per acre – or a population of 7500 to 15,000 in a 250 acre neighbourhood.

.

If the density of development in North Toronto, the most modern section of the city, may be regarded as a reasonable standard, then we may aim to achieve a similar standard in the development of the present housing program. To produce 50,000 houses may therefore be regarded as a community planning program for the creation of about 25 neighbourhood communities, each containing a population of about 7500 people living in about 2000 housing units (3.75 persons per household). (Carver 1948, 39–40)

Carver then went on to show ancillary uses that would be necessary for such a neighbourhood: one public school, one high school for every five neighbourhoods, three acres of playground space for youngsters, 30 acres of playing fields, and retail shops. He set the course for a long tradition of planning new communities by number.

Carver's dream was to create new cities in the suburbs – indeed, that was a title of his 1962 book on suburban planning, in which, he wrote some years later, 'I tried to define which elements of community life should constitute the town centre and how this would provide a starting point for organizing a full social mix in each new off-spring community, so as to avoid having ghettos of middle class blandness in the suburbs and ghettos of poverty remaining in the central city' (Carver 1975, 157).

Hancock treated the idea of neighbourhood very seriously, not simply as a planning device but as the ordering force in contemporary society. He wrote at the time:

The neighbourhood unit in each case is composed of all the elements which go toward making the elementary school the cultural focus. It is felt that with our present day approach to living, the congregating factor of people who live in groups tends to be the elementary school with its related community activities such as adult education groups, cultural study groups, hobby and horticultural groups, ect. ... To that end the physical plan developed locates the school at the centre of each neighbourhood, the residential street system focusing toward the school with its related playground and open space. Residents will then be conscious of their neigh-bourhood identity in the overall scheme of the town. (Hancock and Lee 1954, 3)

While each neighbourhood would have an elementary school, church, and local store, community facilities were located at the central nexus, surrounded by a ring road. Within the ring were the more regional uses – a shopping centre, a high school, a post office, a community and recreation centre, and a library. Places for people to work – this was to be a self-sufficient community – were set at the periphery of the site.

The second defining element of the plan was the road sys-tem. Like other North American cities, Toronto's street system was set in a more or less regular grid pattern. Site conditions sometimes dictated roads that were at odds with the grid, al-though in many cases the grid system rolled on regardless of topography. Only Rosedale, an expensive community in the Garden City tradition, planned in the 1880s but built after the turn of the century, shunned the grid. Hancock chose as an alternative a discontinuous road system of curving streets that ended in T intersections.

A system of short curving roads permitted planning to take account of topography, but Hancock wanted to do more. He wanted to define a distinct style, to give Don Mills an image entirely different from the existing city. Most of the site was flat table land that would have readily succumbed to the grid: instead, an intricate system of curving roads was laid out, en-suring that this was not a community a stranger could hope to drive through leisurely. The discontinuity of the roads meant that the community was closed to outsiders, with the same exclusive cachet that had attached to suburbs built on the outskirts of Italian cities in the eighteenth century.

The road system led directly into a third planning principle – that this should be a community suffused with green space. Green topography was protected by the road layout: ravines were skirted, as were stands of mature trees. But the emphasis on green space as a major design element was achieved in

Don Mills site plan. With the topography evident, there is no correlation between the curvy streets and the lie of the land. Several years later, additions were made to the northwest and northeast, both with a similar road plan of looping streets that create a maze off the main arterials. Hancock and and Lee 1954

other ways as well. Roads were not bordered by sidewalks, but by grassy ditches that stretched into a front lawn leading directly to the house. The result was a countrified air: the road seemed like an intrusion into an otherwise natural setting.

Further, an internal walkway system, permitting pedestrian access throughout the community while avoiding conflict with vehicle-carrying roads, was bordered by greenery and park space. Parks themselves were plentiful, occupying almost 20 per cent of the site. Residential uses, in comparison, occupied not quite twice as much land.

The fourth planning principle, which emphasized the green aspect of the plan, was the approach Hancock took to house design. In North York the standard lot was 25 feet by 140 feet deep. The house was usually much deeper than it was wide and was built close to the street, leaving a large yard at the rear. Most homes were two or two and a half storeys and a driveway would often be shared with an abutting property. One could understand a planner wanting to use a different lot configuration to ensure distinct ownership of the land servicing the family car and to permit a siting more attuned to natural light. But Hancock had a different rationale for his lot layout, as he explained in 1954:

For single family houses, lots are designed wider and less deep than is usual in most subdivisions. In the opinion of the designer, elbow room is a desirable characteristic and allows for increased spacial interests and an ability to site houses both broadside to the street and with the narrow dimension to the street. In many subdivisions, too, the rear portion of the lots is poorly maintained and a burden to the homeowner. The more square lot gives insulation between houses ...

Because the houses are small, open planning has been encouraged in order to increase the visual space within the units. Individual lot widths have been made an average of 60 feet in order that more space will be provided between the housing units. With more land immediately surrounding the houses, design sitings were directed toward a better use of this land and a closer contact with the land. (Hancock and Lee 1954, 3ff)

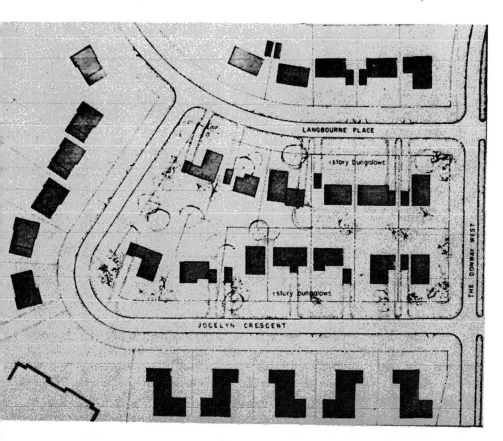

Houses in Don Mills have diverse setbacks from the street, at great variance
from traditional city streetscapes where buildings shared a common relationship to the street. The same random feeling is achieved with apartment
structures in Don Mills. Hancock and Lee 1954

Elbow room and closer contact with the land might not be respectable planning principles – they are somewhat jejune – but they did result in large lots that emphasized the green space already present in the lavish park dedication and pedestrian walkways. The large lot with a single storey house set broadside to the street was what set Don Mills apart from other communities in the city.

It would be a mistake to assume Don Mills was mostly single family structures in a poor man's imitation of Frank Lloyd Wright's ranch-style house. Hancock's community was a mixture of residential forms. Of the 8121 units eventually built in Don Mills, 4501 were apartments, most in three-storey structures that adhered to the thirty-five-foot height limit imposed by the township council across North York. The remaining residential units were a mixture of singles, semi-detached, and row houses, with singles predominating.

Further, Hancock wanted a mix of incomes, and accordingly he planned for a mix of tenures, both ownership and rental. Semi-detached units were specifically planned to be rented, using government subsidies to ensure the new community had its fair share of low-income families.

As it turned out, the income mix desired by Hancock was frustrated by the development's very success. The two-bedroom units planned to serve lower-income factory workers were blocked by North York Council as too modest, and Taylor decided not to fight back. Negotiations to rent houses to Central Mortgage and Housing, which in turn would allocate them to low-income families, were broken off without agreement: CMHC would pay monthly rent no higher than $67.50 and Taylor would go no lower than $75. In the end, Taylor rented them privately for $100 per month.

The fifth planning principle involved land use. Hancock's plan included nonresidential uses – commercial, institutional, and industrial – mimicking a complete and self-sufficient community. Traditional city design had shown a mix of uses, arterial streets often being lined with retail outlets above which were apartments. Offices and sometimes industrial uses intermingled with retail, and planning decisions often involved a sorting of these different and sometimes conflicting uses. Hancock's community ensured there was no possibility of conflict: the uses were clearly separated from each other. That separation even applied to types of residential uses, as Hancock planned for each block to contain only one type of residential use.

The distribution of land use was as follows:

schools 85 acres
churches 16
parks (including private golf course) 400
residential 800
commercial 75
industrial 320
public utility 44
street allowances (including railways) 320
total 2060

The plan called for a population of 29,000, a figure close to Carver's ideal of 7500 in each of four neighbourhoods, and this population was reached by the time residential development was completed in 1963, ten years after construction began. The population was served by eight elementary and three secondary schools, as well as nine churches.

Inside the ring road that looped around the Don Mills/Lawrence intersection, thirty-six acres were devoted to a single-storey regional shopping centre (a planned second storey was not built), curling rink, and hockey arena. North of Lawrence, the area within the ring road consisted entirely of small apartment buildings. Seventeen acres were reserved for corner stores throughout the development, but since the low residential densities made these uneconomical (there simply weren't enough customers for them), retail tenants could never be found and the land was used for residential purposes.

The 320 acres of industrially designated land contained 2.5 million square feet of space, with a floor space index of 0.2, permitting the factories to be set among a sea of grass and trees. Employees totalled 4500. The attempt to create a new town where people lived and worked – the hope was that half

Ortho Pharmaceutical building, in the Don Mills industrial area. John B. Parkin Associates, Architect. Bureau of Architecture and Urbanism 1987, 58–9

the workforce would come from Don Mills – turned out not to square with how people wanted to live their lives, perhaps because housing prices in Don Mills were so expensive that factory workers could not afford to live there. Indeed, only 5 per cent of the jobs were held by local residents.

The private golf course occupied 140 acres, and the remaining 240 acres of parkland were available for residents. A neighbourhood park was adjacent to every school, and the community was laced with walkways edged with green. The small lake planned for the northeast quadrant was never built because of damming of the Don River done upstream.

As *Architectural Forum* declared, 'The new town of Don Mills is a planner's dream coming true' (June 1954, 148). It was a plan on a scale barely imagined by Clarence Stein, embodying all the best thinking of the past few decades.

While Hancock delivered innovations in land-use planning, it was Taylor's skills as an entrepreneur and developer that made the plan so very successful. Just as Hancock's handiwork embodied a radical new approach to urban design, Taylor came up with radical new concepts in land development that ensured the spread of this new urban form.

Don Mills introduced two important innovations from past subdivision and development practice. One dealt with land sales, the other with servicing. Taylor had recognized since Wrentham Estates that the key to maximizing profits was to control land prices so his company, rather than others, would gain any increment in value. For industrial lots the matter was simple: Taylor's company maintained a first option to repurchase for twenty years and required that if construction was not begun within three years of purchase, then the land would revert to his company at the original selling price.

The situation was more complex in regard to residential land, not only because there were many more players but also because repurchase clauses would be unattractive to the home-owners Taylor wished to attract. His hope to have one contractor build all houses was not possible – there simply wasn't a large enough company to undertake work on that scale – and Hancock and his crew wanted a number of builders involved to ensure some diversity of design.

Taylor hit on a way to control small builders that they would find advantageous. A builder would buy a number of lots, paying 25 per cent down and the balance in eighteen months. This minimized cash-flow problems for the contractor providing he built and sold immediately, and it permitted Taylor to re-enter if construction was delayed. As well, if progress was not satisfactory, the contractor would not be permitted to purchase lots the next year.

The scheme was eminently workable and some fifty contractors were involved in building Don Mills. Taylor provided a large-scale model so builders could jointly market their products, and a mobile trailer ensured that the model could be moved across the site as construction proceeded.

Taylor's plan to control land prices to his benefit worked well. House prices jumped from a low of $12,500 in 1953 to $17,000 by 1956. The raw price of land spiralled as well, and in spite of his earlier promise to sell at cost, Taylor was able to sell land he had purchased for $500 an acre, to the school board for $6000 an acre.

Servicing arrangements were more complicated. Municipal councils were wary of large scale new developments in the years following the war because of the large amounts of money involved. In 1950 North York Council followed the growing practice of requiring developers to pay the costs of internal servicing, thus removing that burden from its taxpayers' shoulders. (A comparable arrangement had been followed for both Thorncrest Village and Humber Valley Village.) That still left the biggest questions unresolved: how to fund the needed water and sewage services off- site. North York had no surplus water supply and did not want to finance trunk water lines on its own. Nor did the municipality wish to fund a sewage treatment plant, even if its consultant Faludi argued that the assessment balance of the development would be satisfactory to raise any sums required.

Taylor struck a daring deal. His company would pay the $1.25 million for a sewage treatment plant that was ultimately built on the Don River where the lake had been planned. As for the water service, the company would buy North York bonds to finance the trunk lines, putting funds in escrow in the unlikely that event the taxes raised were insufficient to meet the payments required.

Quite simply, Taylor agreed to assume almost all the servicing costs. The financial risks were taken off the shoulders of the municipality and borne by the developer. The municipality's role of providing services was eschewed for one of simply being a planning regulator. Since the municipality bore little risk, it had little reason not to permit the developer to do exactly as he saw fit. In one simple stroke, Taylor had totally changed the rules of development. Now, the only developers municipalities need concern themselves with were those large enough to provide funds for all services demanded by the municipality.

At the same time, the municipality shed its active involvement in the land development process and became nothing more than a passive rubber stamp able to demand whatever it wanted from developers in return for giving them a free hand to proceed with any plan they thought they could implement. The question of good planning became intricately intertwined with corporate success rather than public goals and objectives. By a strange twist in power arrangements, Hancock's Don Mills was the first and last example in Canada of a plan proceeding because it was thought to be 'good planning.' Henceforth, approval seemed more a function of paying servicing costs the municipalities demanded, and because developers thought they had something they could market.

It should be noted that Taylor also had some effect on the aesthetics of the project. He disliked blue shingles, and they were excluded from the scheme. 'I don't like blue roofs because blue fades,' he is reported to have said. 'Blue is also a bad colour in the sun' (Rohmer 1978, 209).

Don Mills was an immediate success. It had an exclusive cachet that appealed to the upwardly mobile young families that were a product of the postwar booming economy. Houses sold as fast as they could be produced, and Taylor quickly realized the money-making potential of this kind of development. In 1955, when Don Mills was only in its second full year of construction, he purchased 6000 acres of land to the west of Toronto where, a decade and more later, he would again pursue the dream of the modern suburb (now known as Erin Mills), although this time on a much larger scale.

The idea of Don Mills was quickly picked up by other developers. They used the corporate approaches Taylor had refined and the physical plan Hancock had produced. Within a few years, the fringes of Toronto and other Canadian cities began to sprout the progeny of Don Mills, with ring roads, neighbourhoods in each quadrant, walkways, large lots, and town centres. By the 1970s the planning of every Canadian city was dominated by the suburban form espoused by Hancock. With the success of Don Mills in the mid 1950s, the age of the modern corporate suburb had arrived.

4

After
Don Mills

Don Mills was the beginning of almost two decades of experimentation with development on the green fields of the countryside and with redevelopment of the older sections of the developed city. Experiments during this period involved not just new ways of laying out sites, with different kinds of road systems, but also new kinds of building forms, such as high-rise apartment towers and stacked townhouses. The redevelopment of downtown neighbourhoods attempted to incorporate desires for social change, as though the new planning could, *sui generis*, bring about a new social order. New office complexes provided a radically different tone to the look and feel of the city's commercial centre. On the fringes of the city, planners tried to create a brave new world.

Hancock's Alternative to Don Mills

After Don Mills, Macklin Hancock turned his fertile mind to the creation of land-use plans for other new communities. His next major commission was a plan for a site of several hundred acres just to the south of Don Mills. He proudly summed up his approach to this development, Flemingdon Park: 'We do not have any real experience with developments of this kind, conceived and planned on this scale. We do not really know what is going to happen. We do not know whether couples or families with children will find this community a desirable place to live' (Gertler 1968, 205). He was not so much being self-deprecating – the community he was proposing had no like in Canada – as paying due obeisance to one of the most popular values of the day, newness. Nothing was more likely to peak the imagination of a crowd in the 1950s than the thought of doing something that had never before been tried, as though every new step was an experiment with unknown results. This, of course, was one of the underpinnings of modernism, although from the safety of retrospect permitted by thirty years the recklessness of such an approach is shocking. What is meritorious about building something people might not like, something that might not work? What if an engineer had made the same statement at the ribbon-cutting of a bridge he had designed?

Flemingdon Park, model, showing the smorgasbord of building types. The road sweeping to the right is the Don Valley Expressway, requested by E.P. Taylor and agreed to by Metro Council in 1953 at first meeting. Metropolitan Toronto Reference Library

Flemingdon Park, Hancock said, was 'an unparalleled opportunity ... for a completely new type of model community'
(Gertler 1968, 214), although some think he was following
precedents of Roehampton in London and Vallingby in Sweden
(van Nostrand, unpublished). The goal, according to Hancock,
was to create 'a new community of much more urban character, correcting in part the formless sprawled peripheral sectors
of the Metropolitan Toronto area. It is hoped that it can also
act as an example that will turn at least a large segment of our
population back towards the city, as opposed to non-city or
suburban life' (Gertler 1968, 206).

On the 400-acre site, Hancock proposed almost 5000 units, for
a gross density more than three times as great as Don Mills.
Like Don Mills, Flemingdon was planned in neighbourhoods
that clustered around elementary schools, but there were no
single-family houses on spacious lots. Instead, 60 per cent of the
units were in apartment towers twelve and sixteen stories high.
The rest of the units were in smaller apartment buildings,
row houses, and townhouses grouped together over parking
garages:

A serious attempt will be made to produce a completely mixed form
of development with town and row houses, terrace and maisonette
units, high-rise slab and tower apartments and point blocks. Where
possible, underground parking is to be employed to conserve land
for open and activity space, and relieve the landscape of the ever-
present automobile. (Gertler 1968, 219)

Given the use of point and slab towers, much of the site was
devoted to a similar expanse of greenery as seen in Don Mills.
But the idea of discrete units with their own private space, with
individual front and back yards, was nowhere to be seen. Nor
was there a direct link between the individual units and public
space that was usually expressed in the front walk. Instead, a
communal feel pervaded the development. Units in the apartment towers shared long corridors. Townhouses shared winding walkways and common open space, with no clear distinction in the land that belonged to each unit. Parking arrange-

Flemingdon Park building types: point apartment tower, slab apartment tower, and garden apartment housing. Experimentation seems to be more important than comfort. Metropolitan Toronto Reference Library

ments were also communal, in underground garages that served as the foundation of the townhouses.

Hancock carried his ideas of experimentation right into the units, almost asking, as did the planners of Peterlee, that people behave differently. He noted: 'The primary function of private family living is recuperation. The main purpose of modern residential living is informal relaxation and recuperation from the demands of the world of work upon the head of the household and the demands of family life upon his spouse' (Gertler 1968, 224). This statement echoes Le Corbusier's claim that the house is a 'machine for living,' and refers back to the nineteenth-century severing of home and workplace, now treating the former as the place of recuperation from the latter.

The Flemingdon Park project, begun in 1958, did not fare as well economically as Don Mills. While it gained strong adherents among those who designed government-sponsored public housing, it rarely found acceptance in the private market that had already settled on Don Mills as the model of the new city.

Regent Park, Don Mills, and Flemingdon Park differ considerably in detail but share common design characteristics that defined the modernist style of the new city: a surfeit of open green space; a reliance on pedestrian walkways; a rejection of traditional housing forms even though higher density forms had been in existence for hundreds of years; a separation of uses; and a shunning of the grid street pattern in favour of looping discontinuous roads. All are expressions of that underlying set of values now known as the modern suburb. All remained within the framework Ebenezer Howard, Frank Lloyd Wright, Le Corbusier, and Clarence Stein had laid out: they were entirely different from the traditional city of mixed uses set on a grid road system.

Public Housing in the Modernist Vein

This new development style found expression in numerous publicly sponsored housing projects of the 1950s. The push came from Central Mortgage and Housing Corporation, which purchased land on the outskirts of Toronto for several projects.

The total number of units constructed was not large – 3600 units in the decade of the 1950s, which was less than 1 per cent of the units built by the private sector during the same period – but it was influential in terms of design. The design architect at CMHC was Ian Maclennan, whose influcence, working either with his staff or in conjunction with local architects, is clearly visible in the Toronto area.

Four projects – Lawrence Heights, O'Connor Heights, Scarlett Woods, and Warden Woods – were built on the city's outskirts during the 1950s. All share the general characteristics of Lawrence Heights, a 100-acre site north of Lawrence Avenue West, now bisected by the ditch of the William R. Allen Roadway (commonly known as the Spadina Expressway). The density is ten units per acre, and even though that density could easily be built as detached houses on thirty-foot lots, many units are located in three-storey walk-up structures. Others are in row houses, set in blocks of six or eight units, and still others in four-storey apartment buildings.

The original plan was by CMHC architect George Wrigglesworth and included twelve-storey cruciform buildings in the Le Corbusier style. Jack Brown, then a provincial official responsible for intergovernmental housing projects, remembers walking on the site before construction and noticing jets flying overhead towards a landing at nearby Downsview airport. As a former pilot during the Second World War, he took an interest in the planes and decided to make an aerial view of the project site. He made the flight from the Island Airport in early September 1954, on the very day Marilyn Bell was swimming across Lake Ontario, and he recalls the flotilla of boats as she approached the Canadian National Exhibition grounds. As a result of the flight it was recognized that Lawrence Heights was too close to Downsview airport to permit high buildings and, even though working drawings for the towers – since transmuted from cruciforms to slabs – had been completed, it was agreed they could not be built. Instead, three- and four-storey structures were commissioned.

As in Flemingdon Park, there was an attempt to leave most of the site vacant and to experiment with housing forms. Only a small percentage of units are in traditional house-form struc-

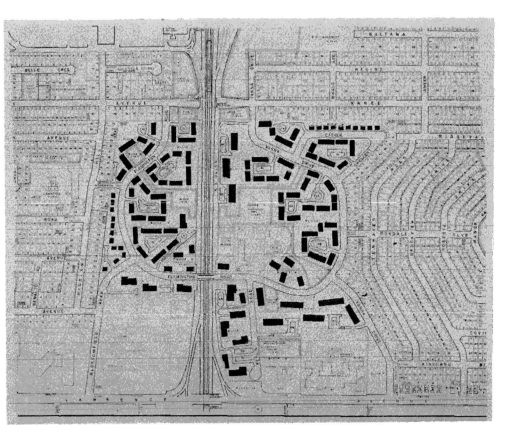

Lawrence Heights. Project buildings are shown in black, and they consist of a mixture of two-storey row houses in blocks of six and eight units, and three-storey walk-up apartments. Most of the buildings are clustered around culs-de-sac, leaving the great majority of the site vacant. An expressway slices through the middle of the project: traditional suburban subdivisions abut the north, east, and west. Based on maps from City of North York Planning Department

tures: these are set on the eastern boundary of the site, and apparently were developed as a 'cordon sanitaire' to meet the objections of neighbouring owners who tried unsuccessfully to prevent this development from being built.

The predominant feel of Lawrence Heights is of housing overwhelmed by grass. Buildings float in a sea of green and seem loosed from any relationship to the street. Densities that are already low compared with the built city appear to be even lower. Complicated looping road systems provide only limited accessibility, creating a feeling of being cut off from local surroundings. It is apparent from the many social problems evident in each project during the last two decades (particularly in Lawrence Heights) that the designs leave much to be desired. As experiments, they could hardly be called successful.

The style also found its way into the extension of Regent Park, which was underway in 1955 as Regent Park South. The essence of the plan is seen on the cover of the redevelopment study. The bottom half of the cover shows two boys fighting on a dirty street bounded by grimy two-storey decaying houses. A few kids sit on the stoops of these decrepid buildings, watching their friends do one another harm, while other kids are involved in acts of vandalism. It is a scene of unrelenting sin and degradation, mostly brought on by an old and oppressive environment. The top half of the cover, by contrast, shows what was expected to happen through the benefits of modern planning and design. The foreground is taken up with a pathway leading to a sylvan glade where children happily play baseball in the comforting shade of a large tree. In the background are the new welcoming homes, including townhouses and a slab-style apartment tower. Redevelopment would provide a new and better world.

There was a sense of mission about the task planners saw before them, a mission caught well by planner Stanley Pickett in 1957:

It is no light task to undertake demolition of people's homes and places of business, to replan large areas, causing widespread disruption and interference with city streets and existing utilities, to

rehouse families in new housing projects and to relocate those
displaced, for whom new housing is not available for one reason or
another. This process must be one of the most difficult operations
which has ever been successfully carried out in the field of human
living and environment, ranking with the tremendous problems
posed by war, by famine, and by refugees and by other large scale
dislocations of the prevailing pattern of life. Nevertheless, our cities
must be renewed; for if they are not, the blight spreading at the
centre will slowly and insidiously strangle the efficiency of the city
and may eventually render it unable to carry out its functions ...
The next ten years present a unique opportunity to Canadians to
use the available skilled labour force for the recreation of worn-out
areas and the construction of housing for persons displaced.
(Pickett 1957, 131)

It was as though the planners had no choice but to do this
dirty deed: to tear down communities, to displace people, in
order to save the people and the city.

   The Regent Park South study, undertaken by social activists
in Toronto, included a proposed plan drawn by Romano
Chukowitz of the province's Community Planning Branch,
Department of Municipal Affairs. Existing buildings and the
street system would be obliterated, as had occurred in Regent
Park North. In their place, new townhouses, maisonettes, and
medium-rise apartment buildings (probably eight storeys high)
would be built surrounded by a sea of green. The total number
of units proposed was 726, an increase from the 458 units
(containing 638 families) then on the site. On 26.5 acres, that
was a density of about thirty units per acre – high in comparison with other city developments. But the floor area ratio –
0.72 times coverage of the land – was quite low.

   The report made a point of arguing against high-rise buildings. Citing the common rationales for high-rise apartments –
land costs and suitability for prospective tenants – it argued
that 'none of these pressures need compel an all-apartment
scheme in Regent Park South' (City of Toronto Planning Department 1955, appendix III, 4). The report also derided the
high-rise structure as 'the architectural dogma insisted upon

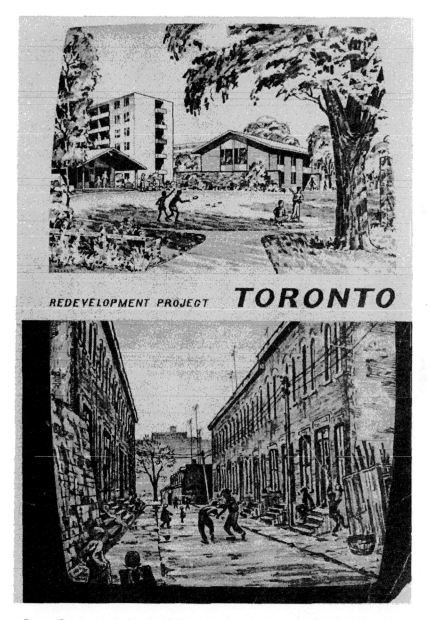

REDEVELOPMENT PROJECT **TORONTO**

Cover, Regent Park South study. The contrast between the disastrous social implications of the nineteenth-century city and the beneficence of modernism is all too obvious. Metropolitan Toronto Reference Library

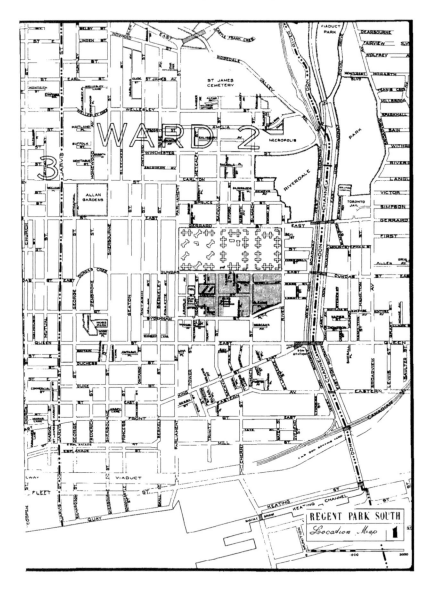

Site of Regent Park South. The cruciforms – appearing almost as a cemetery –
mark Regent Park North, and Regent Park South is indicated in the adjacent
shaded area. Regent North denies the consistency of the grid street pattern in
this part of the city; the same fate will befall Regent South. Metropolitan
Toronto Reference Library

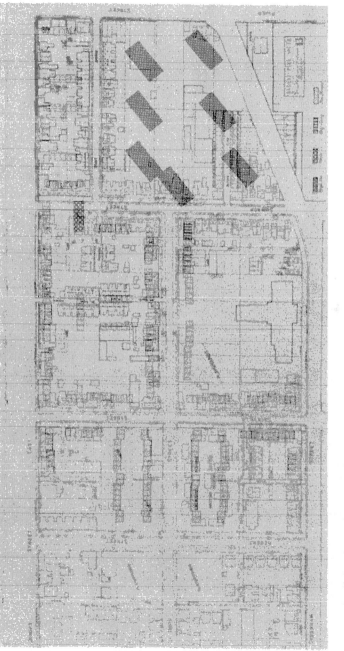

Regent Park South, preliminary plan, 1955. With the exception of Regent Street, the existing street plan and the buildings that lined those streets are obliterated, to be replaced with houses set well back from the street, along the walkways and culs-de-sac. City of Toronto Planning Department 1955

in spite of its unfavourable effects on costs or livability' and continued: 'Elevator buildings are more expensive per square foot of internal space, both to build and to operate. They sacrifice important opportunities for normal self-reliant living by tenants with children. There is an absolute limit to the number of families that can be put on an acre of ground, no matter how tall the buildings' (4). This is a rare instance of the new planning being criticized because it didn't serve the needs of those who would live there. It would take another decade before this approach gained some respectability.

In the end, the advice in the report was not followed, and three schemes that included different mixtures of high-rise buildings and row houses were reviewed. A proposal by J.E. Hoare, architect of Regent Park North, was also discussed: it showed six-storey cruciform buildings marching across the site. In the end, a compromise fifth scheme was recommended: row houses and eight-storey buildings with two-thirds of the units located at grade.

Once there was agreement to proceed with the redevelopment, the plan was considerably modified. Responsibility for planning was assumed by Ian Maclennan, who had just been hired by CMHC, and he retained Peter Dickinson of the Toronto architectural firm Page and Steele to design the apartment structures (Freedman 1990, 16). Hoare designed the townhouses. Maclennan decided to abandon through streets in favour of looped dead-end streets, thus discouraging traffic not related directly to the project. Rising above the rows of townhouses were five fourteen-storey apartment towers set around a central park known as Saints' Square.

In Regent Park South the towers seem to be placed randomly, with reference neither to Dundas Street nor to the boundaries of the newly created square. However, they were carefully arranged to run with the hands of the compass, either directly north/south or east/west. It is a good example of planning with regard to factors that have little relationship to the actual environment.

The interior design of the towers was innovative, replicating ideas Le Corbusier had used in Unité d'habitation in Marseilles.

Regent Park apartment tower. In the middle of the balcony wall is a small box containing a hammer to be used in the event of fire to break into your neighbour's apartment. Charlotte Sykes

Many of the apartments were built on two floors, with an internal stair connection. This permitted units to front on both sides of the building, providing for cross-ventilation. It also meant that corridors were only required for every second floor. Most units were large, with two or more bedrooms, making for a high child count. While this design won the Massey silver medal (Canada's most prestigious design award) in 1958, it was resented by residents who found the building most difficult to live in, often joking about how it was possible to 'fall down the stairs' in their own apartment unit.

The strangest element of the tower design was the fire-escape arrangements. Small balconies were built giving an exterior access to adjoining units. In case of fire, the tenant would make for the balcony, which would provide an exit through the next unit, providing entry was possible. For that purpose, a small box was built on each balcony with a glass front. The glass would be broken and inside would be a hammer, which would be used to break the neighbour's window, providing escape.

The Regent Park South development was important in two ways. First, it made a conscious attempt to provide a diversity of housing forms – some even experimental. There had been variations in building forms in Don Mills, but only of a minor nature, since nothing more than three or four storeys was built. The new diversity of form was picked up with a vengeance in Flemingdon Park and Regent Park South, as well as being integrated into larger planning principles for the urban area as a whole. Second, Regent Park South made it clear that Regent Park North was not an isolated exception. New city building would proceed on two fronts: on undeveloped land in the suburbs and on built-up land that required redevelopment. The two Regent Parks set the stage for an active urban renewal program that planners and civic officials saw as both necessary and beneficial.

The Shopping Plaza

Accompanying these new styles in residential development were new styles in nonresidential development. In 1951 Taylor had built one of Canada's earliest shopping plazas, the York Mills Plaza, at York Mills and Bayview. The plaza at Eglinton and Bayview was contemporaneous, followed shortly by the Don Mills Plaza and then plazas everywhere.

Faludi himself had undertaken designs for several plazas on behalf of developer Sam Sorbara (see 75). His plaza designs differed only in detail from those being planned in almost every suburb. The general principles were threefold. First, the plaza would be entirely commercial: residential uses would be excluded. The traditional mix of uses – the apartment over the store – was abandoned, repeating the moves made three or four centuries earlier to separate workplace from residence. This separation quickly became the norm rather than the exception.

Second, the plaza was developed at a low density. Invariably buildings were one storey, and parking lots were generously surrounded by grass and plantings. While the size of the asphalt parking lot made it difficult to disguise a plaza as a hanging garden, attempts were made to give the plaza the same look as the neighbouring residential community, sharing the love of greenery.

Third, the plaza was designed to cater to the shopper who drove. Shops were set in the centre of the site, ringed with parking spaces. While in communities like Don Mills a pedestrian walkway was designed to permit access to the plaza by foot, the walk across the extensive parking lot was not designed to be a pleasant experience. In most plazas the only walk the shopper was expected to make was from the car to the sidewalk hugging the shops. There was no interior common space in the plaza: the idea of the interior mall was not fully realized until Yorkdale Plaza was developed in the early 1960s.

Putting shops in the middle of the site rather than at the edge also ensured that shoppers were a captive audience: they could visit these particular shops, but to compare what was offered here to what might be offered at other shops took considerable effort. One tradition of strip shopping was that shoppers could easily compare goods, prices, and services: in the new plaza, opportunities for comparison were limited. The owner of the plaza could demand rents on the basis of restricting the number and kinds of stores, setting a mix that would produce maximum returns in terms of sales, the basis on which rents were calculated. Thus plaza design, however unconsciously, was a strong force to limit competition in the marketplace.

Examples of this new style of retail development were not to be found in the built-up city until the 1970s – and then only infrequently. The cost of land discouraged developers with dreams of one-storey buildings and large parking lots. However, the office equivalent of the planning concepts expressed in Don Mills, Flemingdon Park, and Regent Park South finally came downtown in the late 1950s.

Commercial Redevelopment

The challenge facing planners redesigning the downtown business district are expressed well in the American magazine, *Architectural Record*:

The principle difficulty with today's sky-city is the ground-city below, where confusion, congestion and aesthetic chaos prevail. In the city, any open space with a touch of green is a blessing ... If city usefulness and amenities are to be reborn, future planning must extend beyond concern with the plaza or block and must encompass entire street patterns or indeed whole multi-block and neighbourhood developments. Therein lies the future. (Horneck 1961, 2)

The contrast of existing congestion and diversity with the opportunity for clarity and simplicity became more evident in the 1950s. Planners designed for the latter, as though it were the wave of the future. The caption on a photograph of a glassed tower in downtown Manhattan captured the new mood: 'Between the squatting disjointed building masses of lower Manhattan, the narrow diaphragm of the Chase Manhattan Bank rises like a vision of the future' (Hohl 1968, plate 1)

In 1958 the first significant example of the new planning was underway in downtown Toronto – the William Lyon

Mackenzie Building on Adelaide Street one block east of Yonge Street. The location, as it turned out, was a wrong guess: rather than expanding east across Yonge Street, the downtown expanded westerly from the King and Yonge Street intersection, leaving this complex isolated until the late 1980s when high land prices west of Yonge Street sent developers looking for less expensive land to the east.

This complex has all the characteristics of the new planning. The first order of business, as had been the case for the Regent Parks, was land clearance. This site contained several buildings of significant architectural interest, including the Eighth Post Office, a delicious Second Empire Building standing at the head of Toronto Street. Those interested in Toronto's history protested, but were unable to change the plans. Second, the lanes running through the site were closed to form a super-block, reversing the 200-year trend to subdivide land into smaller and smaller parcels. Third, a structure was designed that had little relationship to what surrounded it. The new building makes no reference to the fact that it sits at the head of Toronto Street. There are no uses at grade that are inviting to pedestrians; indeed, the main entrance to the post office in the easterly tower is off the courtyard rather than off the street.

An interior courtyard is accessible from Adelaide and Lombard streets, but its small fountain and several trees are overwhelmed by the size of the surrounding structure. The attempts to create openness and greenery are not entirely successful, although the signals that this is a clean, uncluttered space are plainly evident.

At more than 570,000 square feet of office space, this was by far the largest single commercial development in Toronto, far exceeding the 1929 Bank of Commerce building that for thirty years had dwarfed other structures in the downtown. It also signalled the coming workplace change as office jobs became the main source of employment for city dwellers. Total office space in downtown Toronto stood at six million square feet in 1945, increasing slowly to ten million square feet in 1960, fourteen million in 1964, and twenty-five million by 1973.

The largest office building in downtown Toronto before the

William Lyon Mackenzie Building, Toronto, 1958. The design makes a
merit of repetition and severity, in contrast with the building it replaced.
Charlotte Sykes

late 1950s was the Prudential Life building at King and Yonge streets, with 350,000 square feet. Indeed, in the next two years the largest structures completed were the Canada Trust building at Yonge and Adelaide Streets, 190,000 square feet; and the Crédit Foncier building (demolished in 1989) at Bay and Wellington streets, 100,000 square feet. The William Lyon Mackenzie Building not only paved the way for more complexes embodying the new ideas about city building, but also provided a radically revised idea of an appropriate scale for office buildings.

As designs for the William Lyon Mackenzie Building were being finalized, controversy surrounded the planning of Toronto's new City Hall. A congested site had been purchased at the northwest corner of Bay and Queen streets, and a local firm, the ubiquitous Mathers and Haldenby, was hired to prepare a plan. That plan was presented in 1955 and called for total clearance in order to create a large paved square, at the head of which would be a chunky slab tower facing south. Teachers (particularly Eric Arthur) and students at the University of Toronto's School of Architecture objected to what they saw as inferior architecture and, after a year of debate, City Council agreed to hold an international competition for a new design.

In 1958 Viljo Revell's design was chosen by the jury from among more than five hundred entries. One jury member was none other than Sir William Holford, who had played a mentor role to Macklin Hancock in the design of Don Mills. Revell's project was a landmark for both architecture and planning in Toronto. The site was cleared. The northern portion was occupied by the New City Hall itself, two curved towers containing 815,000 square feet of office space, between which sat a small clam-shaped council chamber. The remainder of the site was left as a paved plaza and reflecting pool/ice rink. Around the perimeter was a walkway a dozen feet above grade, enclosing the whole plaza and providing a strong definition to the site.

The design specifically ruled out any connection – in design, form, or colour – to the remarkable buildings on either side: the Old City Hall to the east, itself the result of an international

Eighth Post Office, at the head of Toronto Street, demolished in 1957
to make way for moderism in the form of the William Lyon Mackenzie
Building, which also contains a post office. Panda Photography

competition, built in a romantic style at the close of the nine-teenth century; and Osgoode Hall to the west, a complex that has stood as the bastion of the province's legal community and court system since 1845. The New City Hall was to be linked to the future, not to the past.

The New City Hall was controversial, but almost immediately it was publicly lauded as the city's successful leap into the future. While those who work in it complain about the opaqueness of the exterior walls, the building seems to be held in high regard by many Torontonians.

Both the New City Hall and the William Lyon Mackenzie Building, as examples of new planning applied to large office complexes, were the result of government initiatives. They were closely followed by a proposal from a private-sector firm, the Fairview Corporation, working on behalf of the Toronto-Dominion Bank. A merger between the Bank of Toronto and the Dominion Bank took place in 1955. To mark the occasion, the new company decided to build a new head office, and a land assembly ensued surrounding the Bank of Toronto struc-ture at King and Bay streets. It was hoped the whole superblock – Bay, Wellington, York, and King streets – could be purchased and redeveloped as a cohesive site.

Fairview was owned by the Bronfman family, whose extensive holdings included the Seagrams distillery. Through the influ-ence of architect and family member Phyllis Lambert, Mies van der Rohe had been chosen to design the Seagram building in New York. That structure, completed in 1958, represented the latest word in the International Style and gained many plaudits. It made good sense for the company to hire Mies for the Toronto project. The local architects working with him were John B. Parkin and the Bregman & Hamann firm.

The Toronto-Dominion Centre, as the complex of black towers came to be called, required demolition of all the build-ings Fairview had acquired in the superblock, except for a few buildings on the Bay street frontage and at the corner of King and York streets. It included the magnificent Bank of Toronto building on the southwest corner of King and Bay streets. When questioned about this demolition and whether the building

Toronto City Hall proposal. Mathers and Haldenby, 1955. This plan calls for
clearance of a large site and the erection of a slab tower which, at that time,
managed to look old-fashioned, and now seems postmodern. Metropolitan
Toronto Reference Library

Transverse section
Querschnitt

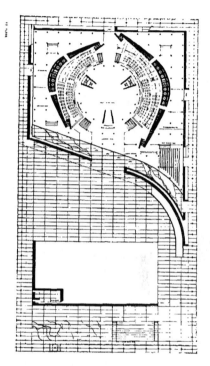

South elevation
Südansicht

The original scheme, 1959
Originalentwurf, 1959

Ground floor plan
Grundriss I. Stock

Toronto City Hall sketches. Viljo Revell, 1959. The contrast with the Mathers and Haldenby plan, particularly the excitement in Revell's approach, is apparent. Metropolitan Toronto Reference Library

could be retained, a Fairview official advised that 'it did not fit in.' As a representative expression of the new planning values, a model of the demolished bank was placed in the new banking pavilion. Concern expressed about the loss of this and other structures in the block was not able to secure any change in the plans.

Laneways throughout the site were closed and sold to Fairview. A plaza – half grass, half concrete – covered the site, on which were placed three black towers and a black one-storey banking pavilion. The structures bore no relationship to surrounding buildings, and the tallest building, the fifty-five-storey Toronto-Dominion Tower, was set as far back from King Street as possible, requiring a long and windy walk across the plaza.

Uses were separated: all office uses were located above grade, and retail uses were below grade in a shopping mall organized along principles comparable with those found in suburban shopping plazas. The density of the project was significant – twelve times coverage of the land – and the office space available totalled 2.5 million square feet, three times larger than the New City Hall.

The Toronto-Dominion Centre was quickly seen as state-of-the-art planning. The idea of clearance and new construction was viewed as the most desirable way to plan the city's future, particularly if a plaza could accompany new tall buildings. Torontonians felt that with the Toronto-Dominion Centre, they had again shown their inclination to be a city of the future.

Metropolitan Planning and the New Suburbs

While new planning ideas found expression in specific projects, they also crept into larger plans for the urban area. Faludi's 1943 master plan for Toronto contained peripheral references to site design. It was followed by the 1949 plan for metropolitan Toronto, which took the same kind of general approach to larger planning questions such as population, land use, transportation, services, and the creation of a green belt. That plan

Toronto-Dominion Centre. Mies van der Rohe, 1962. The purity of form of black towers in a cleared field is a considerable contrast with the crowded complex city of the nineteenth century. Metropolitan Toronto Reference Library

worried about the lack of regional planning control, and suggested that a metropolitan political framework was required – one that was finally enacted in 1953.

Much of the plan concerned itself with the city's expected growth and how that growth would be serviced. It assumed that growth would take a certain form:

In considering the accommodation to be provided for this new population the [Planning] Board is strongly impressed with the necessity of establishing rigid regulations to control densities and urges all municipalities that have not already done so to give this matter very serious attention. The unnecessary crowding of buildings on land has all over the world led not only to unsatisfactory living conditions and eventual depreciation but also is the primary cause of true congestion. (Toronto and York Planning Board 1949, 9)

The report went on to suggest that the maximum persons per net acre for fully serviced land should be thirty, or about eight units per acre, a density comparable to that found in Don Mills. It continued: 'In the case of duplex dwellings and apartment houses, greater densities may be permitted but in any case occupation should be limited to 12,000 persons per square mile' (9).

Given that the city of Toronto, then with a population of 670,000 in thirty-five square miles, had a gross density of 19,000 persons per square mile – and a net density in residential areas of well over 22,000 – the recommendation called for a substantial change. The 12,000 upper limit advocated by the plan is for the most dense residential forms: single-family houses would surely be at densities below 10,000 persons per square mile, or about twenty persons per acre. The plan's supporters were convinced that lower densities resulted in better cities. While the plan adopted the general approach taken by Humphrey Carver in *Housing for Canadians* published in the previous year, it does not use his rationale, which was based on the assumption that North Toronto was well planned. The 1949 plan proceeded on the assumption that lower densities were better.

Shortly after the creation of the Metropolitan Toronto municipal federation in 1953, the Metro Planning Department was formed. Under the leadership of Murray Jones, the new department attracted a number of strong regional planners, including Hans Blumenfeld, who began working out the rudiments of a regional plan. That plan, while serving as a guide for decision making from the late 1960s on, was formally adopted by Metro Council only in 1980. The 'informal' Metro plan covered the same topics as the 1949 plan, but specifically argued for higher densities along suburban transportation routes, providing the same kind of residential mix on a regional scale as Hancock had attempted to provide in Flemingdon Park.

Metro planners assumed that the general plan for Metro would be supported by more local 'district' plans providing a greater level of detail on development opportunities and restraints. District plans would correlate residential densities with school needs, park space, road patterns, and environmental considerations. The district plan was intermediate between the master plan and the community plan.

The first district plan was prepared in February 1962 by Eli Comay, then commissioner of planning for Metro Toronto. It covered District 10, the Jane/Finch corridor area in the northwest part of the metropolitan area. The report accompanying the plan notes:

The plan for District 10 has been prepared as a pilot document, in co-operation with the staffs of the North York Planning Board, the North York Board of Education and the Metropolitan Separate School Board to illustrate the content of district plans within the context of the overall Metropolitan Official Plan and to indicate the function which district plans will perform after adoption of the Metropolitan Official Plan. It should be noted that this district plan has reference to a suburban district which is partially developed and is designed primarily to accommodate new development. (Metropolitan Toronto Planning Board 1962, 22)

The plan deliberately encouraged an urban form in the new style, combining the principles used in Don Mills and Flemingdon

Park, as can readily be seen from the remarks in the covering
report on residential densities and form:

The maximum gross density of 30 persons for the residential land in
the whole district is not regarded as restrictive; in fact it is much
higher than the suburban densities of recent years. It conforms to
the principle in the draft Metropolitan plan that overall densities in
most suburban areas should be raised. In the Official plan densities
are one of the tools which help to distribute the growing population
in a rational way having regard to the planned provision and likely
demand for public services such as transportation, education,
recreation and sewers and water. There are a number of factors
which lead to the conclusion that under present conditions of a free
enterprise housing market – both for rental and purchase accommodation – over a wide suburban area an average density around 30
persons per acre is the upper limit which can be expected during
the next decade or two ...

Apart from multiple family units it is possible to increase residential densities by a more compact form of single family development.
This can happen only by revisions to the zoning by-laws. Although it
is possible that a new single family category may be added to the
existing range which would permit narrower frontages, the use of
such category may be restricted and in any event the increase in
densities would be very slight ...

Finally, emphasis should be laid on the fact that the recommended
maximum densities within each section allow for greater freedom of
choice in actual site densities, ranging from 10 persons or less per acre
to 150 persons and more per acre on specific sites. It is desirable that
the higher densities be achieved by a diversification of housing types
rather than a sharp division between single and semi-detached homes
over most of the area and concentrations of high rise apartments in a
few locations. (Metropolitan Toronto Planning Board 1962, 27–8)

The report spent considerable time arguing for the inclu-
sion of apartments and other kinds of rental accommodation
in the district. It suggested:

To overcome the tendency of establishing a one-sided community in

the suburbs consisting largely of young families, it is desirable to
introduce a variety of dwellings which cater to a wider range of the
community. Second, to achieve higher residential densities which
can support a full range of services and community facilities, multiple housing, including apartments, need to be introduced. A subsidiary reason for apartment buildings – architectural effect and
relief of the monotony of uniform low housing development – is an
important aspect from a civic design point of view. (Metroplitan
Toronto Planning Board 1962, 32)

The report referred to the variety of rental housing forms
in Flemingdon Park, calling it 'a welcome change.' But it rejected the idea of higher densities, even though it recognized
that 'public transportation becomes practical only with densities
higher than those produced by single and semi-detached
houses' (35):

Redevelopment of central city sites, because of high land costs,
inevitably requires high density development. In the suburbs, apart
from some locations, there is no such economic necessity, and a
distribution of multiple housing at medium densities should be the
policy since there is no justification on either planning or social
grounds for very high densities in the suburbs. (Metorpolitan
Toronto Planning Board 1962, 34)

The report assumed widespread agreement on the need for
great amounts of open space around apartments, noting that
'open space considerations in apartment locations require little
explanation' (36), and indeed giving none.

Of the 11,610 acres in District 10, 1348 acres of public and
private open space serve 4858 acres of residential uses and 3828
acres of industrial land. As a ratio to residential uses, open
space is more than 1:4, showing the extent to which planners
assumed the importance of green space.

Thus, at all levels, the new ideas of lower density, more
green space, and variety of housing forms had taken hold.
They were evident at the community, district, and metropolitan
levels. It is particularly ironic that the urban form most dis-

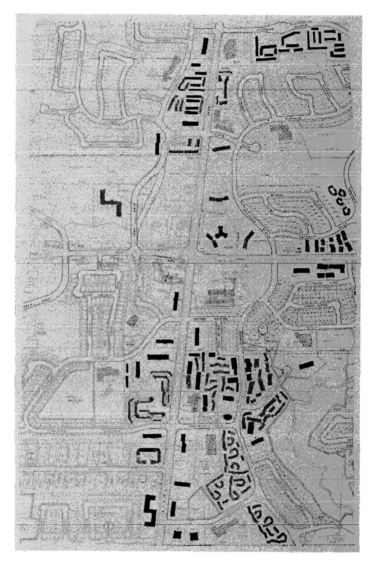

Jane/Finch area, 1990. Multiple-unit residential projects are shown in a dark colour. Slab structures are generally high-rise towers of fifteen to twenty storeys; broken forms are low-rise townhouse projects on private walkways. Schools are indicated by diagonal stripes. Shopping plazas are at the south-east and southwest corners of Jane Street and Finch Avenue, in the centre of the map. The emptiness of the space and the discontinuity of streets and building forms are readily apparent. Based on maps from City of North York Planning Department

cussed and most criticized in Metro Toronto during the 1980s for its inadequacies and the social problems it harbours is none other than the Jane/Finch corridor, which the District 10 plan had tried to make into an ideal community.

The complaints have much to do with the urban form of Jane/Finch: the vast amount of common spaces both inside and outside buildings seems ideal for drug dealing and anonymous crime; the distance of buildings from public streets makes using public transit a most unpleasant experience, although the low income of many Jane/Finch residents leaves them no option but to travel by transit; generally low suburban densities means that transit service is not exemplary, certainly not up to the standards of denser parts of the city; and the high-rise and other multiple unit buildings are inappropriate for the many children living in the area. Other complaints – such as a lack of social services – relate more to the inability of the Jane/Finch community to influence the political system, but that too might be a result of urban form, in that those who can choose to live somewhere more pleasant have made that choice. In the 1980s a Jane/Finch address was considered perhaps the least desirable in Metro Toronto.

The new ideas found further expression in the plan for the newly founded York University, which would occupy a site immediately to the east of District 10. This land had been purchased in the mid 1950s by the federal government in partnership with the provincial government, and in 1962 it seemed so likely to be dedicated for the new university that planning consultants were hired by the Board of Governors. The consultants went by the name UPACE, University Planners, Architects, and Consulting Engineers. It was a consortium of three well-known Toronto firms: Gordon S. Adamson and Associates, Architect; John B. Parkin Associates; and Shore & Moffat and Partners. The consortium made its report in June 1963, a short ten months after it received its commission.

Much debate was taking place in North American circles about the planning of university campuses, given the explosion in the number of students wishing to secure postsecondary education and the great amount of money being provided for new facilities. Almost without exception the new or expanded campuses were planned in the new style. The UPACE report outlined why that was the case for York: 'The intellectual tradition that York renews can best be expressed through those principles underlying much great university architecture of the past, but only in forms appropriate to modern conditions and techniques' (UPACE 1962, 9). The sentiment echoes that on which Howard undertook his Garden City thinking: this is a new age that demands new solutions.

The decision was made immediately that it should be a pedestrian campus, suffused with greenery and open space. Of the 474 acres available, the planners decided to contain most of the building activity to a 130-acre central core surrounded by a ring road, with buildings at a density of 0.68 times coverage – a density lower than could be found in retail strips in Toronto neighbourhoods. Nevertheless, the planners thought they were mimicking the great spaces (and universities) of the world, and photos of St Mark's Square in Venice, Yale University, and a host of other delightful places are sprinkled throughout the plan. The document notes:

The possibility of a pastoral or suburban campus was considered, but the most appropriate qualities are urban: the concentrated activity and intense development of the city.

The buildings should be closely spaced, about paved or planted quadrangles after the example of the old European universities and towns and these quadrangles should be accessible only to people on foot ...

The frequently inclement weather, wind, rain, snow and intense summer sun, make scattered buildings joined by long unprotected walks undesirable. Protection from the weather as well as from motor traffic is necessary if the amenities of the pedestrian zone are to be fully realized.

This protection can best be achieved by closely spaced buildings connected by covered links where possible. In this way a virtue can be made of necessity; a uniquely Canadian solution can be found to the problems created by the Canadian climate. (UPACE 1962, 20)

The plan emphasized the role of the pedestrian – typically a driver emerging from a car in the parking lot at the edge of

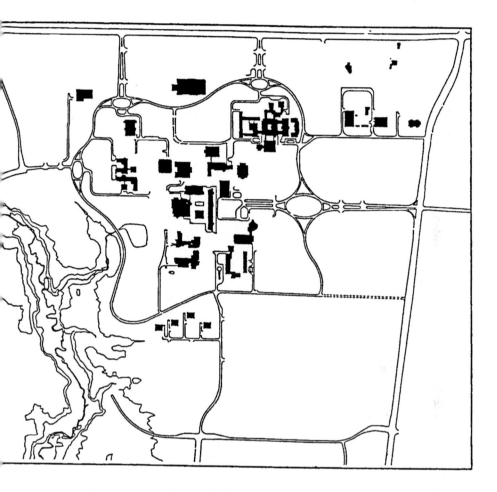

York University site plan, showing roads and buildings in 1988. The discontinuous road system is at its most extreme. The plan contemplated about double the number of structures actually built and shown here.
York University

the campus, since everyone agreed York was to be populated by a student and faculty body of commuters. The plan proposed to eliminate the conflict between cars and pedestrians by simply prohibiting car access inside the ring road bounding the central core: thus the central core was to consist of buildings set on walkways, not on streets. This assumption that buildings should be set in a sea of green grass was no different from that underlying the approach to Lawrence Heights or Regent Park, and it had the same effect of making buildings seem anchorless, without a firm relationship to anything. As the plan notes, without a hint of irony: 'The creation of this [central pedestrian] zone requires a rational circulation system, and the design of buildings without "front" and "back." Pedestrians and vehicles will approach these buildings from opposite sides, the public "face" will be turned away from the centre of the campus' (14).

Considerable thought was given to the variety of building design, and the function of the high rise – certainly not needed to accommodate densities, which in any case were exceptionally low – was to provide that variety: 'High residences offer York University definite advantages in internal organization. They can also provide greater individuality of college design, lower land coverage, variety of silhouette and visual accents of the campus.' The focus for these disparate design elements was to be not a building but an open space, remaining true to the new planning idea that open spaces were better than filled spaces: 'The focal point of the university should be an open space, a great "place" where the university can formally gather on special occasions and casually meet at other times. The central square will be the first in a hierarchy of squares or quadrangles, the termination of the pedestrian paths and the designation for the ceremonial motor approach to the university' (UPACE 1962, 20). The ceremonial approach would be a ramp rising one floor above grade and passing under a bridge in the main administration building. The report noted: 'These [graduation] processions will pass under the long social sciences and humanities building which stands along the east side of the square, symbolically linking the arts and the sciences' (UPACE 1962, 26).

As it turned out, the Canadian climate put an end to dreams of the central square: it is now located in the dark and gloomy first floor of the Ross Building, where glass walls look out at several trees that are captured in a barren courtyard. The walkway system has turned out to be dangerous for pedestrians precisely because there are no cars whose drivers could have provided a modicum of security to those who walk alone. Further, the harsh winter winds (which blow during most of the university term) make walking decidedly unattractive, and the university has created underground walkways between buildings. Some of the blame for these deficiencies have been laid at the feet of those politicians who decided not to fund all of the many buildings the planners counted on being built.

As university officials in the late 1980s reviewed the physical form left them by the planners twenty-five years before, they made two significant moves: they demolished the ceremonial ramp, and they began building a new street system lined with structures inside the ring road. Planning ideas began to come full circle.

5

Rejection of
Modern
Planning

Plan for Toronto waterfront, 1964. A symphony (or dirge) in water, concrete, and steel, with a few trees thrown in for local colour. Toronto Harbour Commission

Early experiments in new-style residential and commercial development met with success. Planners for developers, public
agencies, and governments became bolder in their proposals,
and few qualms were expressed about pushing aside the old to
make way for the new. So many and various were the dreams
for refashioning the city during the 1960s that planners often
assumed they had a free hand.

The public, however, interrupted the reverie in short order
with struggles around commercial proposals – the Old City
Hall, Commerce Court, and Metro Centre – and several neighbourhood urban renewal and redevelopment schemes. By the
time the decade ended in Toronto, new-style planning ideas
has undergone a sharp critique, one they might not survive.
Public sentiment coalesced to challenge the idea that developers and planners could refashion the city to their liking.

One of the few authors in the 1960s who refused to give cre-
dence to the theories of modern planning was Jane Jacobs,
and community advocates avidly read her 1961 book, *The Death
and Life of Great American Cities*. Referring to planning since
Ebenezer Howard, she commented, 'The entire concoction is
irrelevant to the working of cities.' She continued: 'Cities happen to be problems in organized complexity like the life sciences. They present situations in which half a dozen or even
several dozen quantities are all varying simultaneously and in
subtly interconnected ways' (433). This approach was not one
that admired the ideas of pure form and use, or of the need to
separate different uses. It's impact, however, was not felt in
Canada for almost a decade and the 1960s witnessed a succes-
sion of plans in the new mould.

In 1964, for instance, the Toronto Harbour Commission, a
frequent proposer of schemes for its waterfront land holdings,
suggested a modern extravaganza at the foot of Bay Street:
austere building blocks of glass and steel set on a concrete
plaza. Several years later, the American planner and architect
Buckminster Fuller was invited to Toronto, fresh from the
popular success of his geodesic dome at Montreal's Expo 67. He
suggested a large pyramid and block tower for the waterfront,
providing at one blow both the extinction of the old and its

Plan for Toronto waterfront. Buckminster Fuller, 1968. What could more offend – or impress – the sensibilities of Torontonians caring about the city's waterfront than a pyramid? Toronto *Sun*

replacement with new, pure form. Neither scheme moved beyond the proposal stage.

Other plans were much likelier candidates for implementation. Immediately after the Toronto-Dominion Centre was safely under way, a proposal was released to create a large shopping and office complex in the superblock Queen, Bay, Dundas, and Yonge streets. The site would be cleared of all buildings, including the Old City Hall, and large towers set on an open plaza.

Mayor Nathan Phillips had foreseen such a future for this block since March 1955, a few months after his first election as mayor. He dreamed that the Old City Hall could be replaced by something larger and more modern, more fitting to the new Toronto. He hoped his new hall would be funded by selling the old hall as a development site. At one point he asked John David Eaton, owner of Canada's largest department store, which owned land immediately to the north and east, to make an offer (Phillips 1967, 141). Eaton did not respond favourably, and the proposal to build a new city hall for $18 million was not liked by the voters: when asked to approve the idea in the December 1956 election, they demurred.

Looking for other ways to fund his dream, Phillips then hit upon the scheme of bringing the new Metro Council into the picture as a purchaser of the Old City Hall (Phillips 1967, 142). Metro agreed to pay $4.5 million for the old structure and, with that money helping to meet the costs of the new building, voters in the 1957 election approved construction of the new hall. On that basis, the process leading to the construction of Revell's building began (see chapter 4).

As for the Old City Hall, Metro expected the sixty-year-old building would simply continue as the city's main court house; it was surprised when it was immediately offered $8 million for the site by the Eaton company. That offer led to protracted negotiations and consideration of what might be built there. Various schemes were put forward, all calling for clearance of the site and the construction of large towers on a concrete plaza. Some plans suggested the clock tower of the Old City Hall be retained, much like a trinket from the city's former life. One called for a grade crossing of Queen Street over a newly sunken Bay Street.

Not everyone wanted to see the old demolished to make way for the new. 'Friends of the Old City Hall' was the organization of architects, historical building buffs, and others interested in civic affairs that came together to oppose any plan promising to threaten the old masterpiece. The group represented the solid middle-class professional, and knew all the tricks about reading reports, writing to politicians, ferreting out backroom information, and generally making it clear its members would not permit Old City Hall to be demolished without a fight. When debates on the matter occurred, they filled the galleries of city council and they asked politicians to choose sides.

This group turned out to be the key stumbling block to those seeking a firm arrangement for a new development on the site. Metro chairman William Allen, who as a provincial government appointee did not have to face the voters, wished to tear the building down. He was opposed strongly by Toronto mayor Donald Summerville, a populist. When Summerville died suddenly in a charity hockey game, his term was filled by Philip Givens, who agreed with Allen. The Friends had much to do with Givens's defeat at the polls in December 1966 by William Dennison, who was solidly on the side of the conservationists.

On 22 February 1967 the Toronto *Star* reported that the finale to the ten-year struggle was about the occur:

A radical new design for Eaton's downtown department store is under study ...

The building will comprise four six-storey sections tapering slightly toward the top and supporting a two-storey merchandise mart. Ground level between the four sections will be an open pedestrian plaza, and at upper levels the four sections will be connected by glass-walled bridges.

There will also be bridges from the seventh floor to the 50 storey office tower at the head of Bay Street.

For the next few months there were behind-the-scenes negotiations between the developer and Metro officials, and strong protests by the Friends who, though pictured as a gaggle of old ladies in running shoes, were a remarkedly diverse group worried about the past and the future of the city.

During negotiations the plan changed, although the parameters of the dream remained within the new planning ideology. The new scheme saw three large towers of sixty-nine, fifty-seven, and thirty-two storeys, as well as a round 500-room hotel. The *Star* noted, 'All streets in the 20 acre site would disappear, creating what planners call a "superblock." Underneath it would be levels for car parking and pedestrian malls with small shops' (18 May 1967).

On 18 May, however, Eaton's withdrew, indicating it would not proceed. It was difficult to say whether the struggle over the future of the Old City Hall was the turning point, or whether the real problem was that Metro and Eaton's could not agree on the value of the land to be conveyed to Eaton's from the streets it wanted closed.

The newspapers were heart-broken. A *Star* headline on 19th May read, 'Toronto's world image for big-time real estate gone with Eaton Centre.' A story followed lamenting that the scheme was 'something that could have put Toronto in league with the more sophisticated cities in the world.' The Toronto *Telegram* took a similar line, showing the extent to which progress had become tied to the new planning precepts of demolition and replacement:

No other city would have anything to compare with the dimensions and the splendour of it. Not only would it revitalize its own area and add enormously to the civic treasury, it would contribute an immense charge in a chain reaction to the redevelopment of the whole downtown core. No other city would have piled obstacles in the way of this development. Montreal, Pittsburg, Baltimore, any municipality governed by men and women with imagination, foresight, and faith in the future of their country would have seized the opportunity with enthusiasm and given their energies to expedite the plan ...

For there can be no mistaking what they have done. They have set Toronto back years. While Vancouver, Edmonton, Calgary and

Old City Hall, sketches for its demise. The old building was impressive enough
for several plans to be attempted to retain the clock tower, even though it
would be dwarfed by giant structures of various shapes and sizes. One scheme
buries Bay Street under a Queen Street overpass – a really modern idea
invading the city. Metropolitan Toronto Reference Library

Montreal surge ahead with great developments, our councillors talk about setting up barrels in a public place for donations to revive the moribund St Lawrence Centre for the Arts. (20 May 1967)

In the glare of criticism, the aldermen struck committees to revive the development, but nothing came of it.

Indeed, the dream of destruction and replacement was not one that found a comfortable home in downtown Toronto. The Friends had struck a nerve that ran deep. In penance for approving a new arts centre – a lump of concrete in the Brutalist style, replacing elegant nineteenth-century warehouses on Front Street East – the politicians chose, as the city's project to mark Canada's centennial, to strengthen the past rather than obliterate it. Council decided to refurbish the long-abandoned St Lawrence Hall built in the middle of the nineteenth century, and to rebuild the market building that had housed farmers since 1834. The lure of the new may have eradicated a caring for the old in the newspaper community, but not among a majority of city politicians and their constituents.

Those interested in older buildings were one group who struggled against the new style, and the preservation of the Old City Hall gave them an important boost. Henceforth schemes that required wholesale demolition would not have an easy time of it. Modernists had to modify their approach, saving whatever buildings they were required to spare. This influence was clearly recognized in the development proposed by the Canadian Imperial Bank of Commerce on the southeast corner of King and Bay, across the street from the Toronto Dominion Centre.

In 1961 the Canadian Bank of Commerce and the Imperial Bank of Commerce merged to become the Canadian Imperial Bank of Commerce. The merger combined land holdings to produce a significant development site in the Bay/King/Yonge/Wellington block, and the new bank set about to consolidate its holdings. The *Telegram* building at the corner of Bay and Melinda streets was purchased and demolished in 1964, followed a few years later by the ten-storey Eagle Star building. But the bank had problems with land assembly on Yonge Street, and a decision was made to keep the development on the westerly portion of the superblock.

Architects I.M. Pei of New York in conjunction with the Toronto firm of Page & Steele were retained in 1965, and a year later Mayor Philip Givens was hinting that a major development was in the works. Accordingly to a report in the *Globe and Mail* of 29 November 1966 covering a speech by the mayor, 'Mr. Givens used downtown development and the new bank plans (of Canadian Imperial) to show that his vision of a revitalized downtown core wasn't pie in the sky.' He was quoted as saying: 'These are not dreams, they are on the way now. All we need is the kind of administration that doesn't practise negativism.' Givens said a tall building, between eighty and ninety storeys, would be built on the site. He had no idea whether the lavish Bank of Commerce building, built to thirty-five storeys as the highest office tower in the Commonwealth at the depth of the Depression, would remain.

The scheme's proponents must have learned from the fate of the Eaton Centre development. The plans released in August 1968 showed a sleek silver tower alongside the old Bank of Commerce. A decision had clearly been made to compromise the new planning motto of total clearance enough not to provoke those who thought the city's heritage worth keeping.

Other elements of the new planning were evident, however. Above-grade uses were kept entirely to office uses: retail stores were placed below grade. As much open space as possible was retained on the site, with the bank tower set back twenty or more meters from both Bay and King streets, creating a paved windy plaza that all those using the building would have to cross. (Some winter days the plaza is so windy that ropes are strung between the flagpoles to guide visitors into the building and provide them with something to hold onto rather than being swept off their feet.) The new buildings were designed without reference to surrounding structures: the new silver tower seems to regard the older Bank of Commerce with disdain in regard to siting, entrances, and design elements.

The key change was that architects began to recognize that new planning principles could not be implemented holus-bolus

in downtown Toronto. Schemes espousing only those principles would not secure civic approval. At the same time, architects had to look for ways of showing that their proposals fit
within the mainstream of the international movement, and
that seemed to be the case with Commerce Court. As the
Toronto *Star* reported:

Like other real estate experts, [Donald] Kirkup [research director
of the Toronto Real Estate Board] felt the new development would
put Toronto as a leading city on the building map, outstripping
Montreal and many other North American cities.
   'This is the start of the real city of Toronto,' said Harvey Keith of
H. Keith Ltd., realtors. (Toronto *Star*, 1 August 1968)

Commerce Court met with council approval and construction
began in 1969.
   The next major downtown office development was proposed
by the Royal Bank: it opted for a smaller, more distinctive
building fitting tightly on a site that was not a superblock. The
Royal Bank plaza consists of two triangular towers, the higher
a mere thirty-five storeys, with gold-tinted windows. While it
does not eschew the new planning principles – retail shops are
again relegated to the basement – it certainly does not flaunt
them. When, a few years later, plans of First Canadian Place
were released, they showed no at-grade open space to speak
of: the building came to the edges of the sidewalk, and in
some cases even provided a canopy.
   After Commerce Court, but before the reformist principles
had become fully established, the new revisionist mood in the
downtown was tested by the massive Metro Centre development,
which became public fare in 1969. The plan proposed redevelopment of 200 acres of land occupied by railway yards and
tracks. Much of the site was already vacant, save for buildings
facing onto Front Street, including Union Station, which had
been built just after the First World War. These buildings would
be cleared away, making a large site that could be developed
in any conceivable manner. What the Metro Centre proponents
wanted was a development in the new style, one that refused

Commerce Court. The new tower rises right out of this promotion sketch, almost obliterating the Bank of Commerce building that peeks out just behind it. Metropolitan Toronto Reference Library

to recognize the existing street system, one that emphasized large open spaces and buildings in an extreme expression of modernist ideas.

The Metro Centre scheme involved many complicated issues, including land exchanges and related questions, servicing, density and land use, a transportation terminal, phasing, and cost sharing. Many of these issues were resolved to the satisfaction of city council, which approved the scheme in 1972, but a large group of citizens indicated they would contest the development before the Ontario Municipal Board.

The most telling issue was the proposed destruction of Union Station. Like the Old City Hall, Union Station became a rallying point for those who might not have otherwise become involved in the issue of planning the downtown. The building was seen as a superb piece of architecture that had played a large part in the city's social history – it was where soldiers left for the Second World War, and it was the entrance to the city for the hundreds of thousands of immigrants who arrived in the late 1940s and 1950s. That planners and city council would be so cavalier about this structure was something that raised the ire of many – to such an extent that the Ontario Municipal Board refused to approve council's decisions implementing the scheme.

The OMB decision recommending substantial amendments was placed before the newly elected reform council in 1973. New council members demanded that Union Station not be demolished. When a motion to this effect carried council, the developer indicated that this condition put an end to the development. The Metro Centre development proposal was withdrawn – the clearest signal yet that attempts to redevelop the downtown as though the existing city didn't matter would not meet with success. The modernist dream for replanning downtown Toronto had been rejected.

In the residential neighbourhoods surrounding the downtown, the same initial enthusiasm for the modernist vision was followed by opposition and defeat, for both publicly and privately sponsored projects. The apparent success of the radical new plans for Regent Park North and then Regent Park South

Metro Centre plan, 1969, and photo montage. The plan does not allow for through roads or a continuous internal street system. Instead, buildings are placed within their own context, without reference to the surrounding city. The large tower seems like a rocket ready to leave the city for foreign climes.
Metropolitan Toronto Reference Library

was followed by an ambitious program to redevelop many other downtown neighbourhoods, just as the Bruce report had called for in the early 1930s. Older studies were pulled out which showed that many neighbourhoods were deteriorating and, to use Eugene Faludi's terms when he studied Hamilton in the early 1940s, that blight was spreading. The federal government had passed legislation permitting cost-sharing between local, provincial, and federal governments for any urban renewal scheme involving clearance and new construction, or, in some cases, rehabilitation. Urban renewal sponsored under this legislation became the dominant mode for introducing new planning ideas to the city.

The principles governing urban renewal schemes were always the same and did much eventually to make the program unpopular: get rid of the street system; demolish as many buildings as possible; create great chunks of open space; and build functional structures that looked entirely different from everything else.

After Regent Park South, Toronto City Council had to choose which of several proposed urban renewal projects would be next. It decided, in June 1958, to expropriate properties in the Moss Park area and proceed with the construction of half a dozen eighteen-storey buildings. This was a significant change for the area since it called for the closing of the many streets and lanes within the superblock of Shuter, Parliament, Queen, and Sherbourne streets and the demolition of hundreds of two- and three-storey homes. Some 1800 people were to be evicted, but there was little public outcry. Common wisdom was that total demolition was a reasonable step. As the Toronto *Star* noted, 'The recent decision to raze Moss Park's dilapidated buildings is a remedial step in the redevelopment of Toronto's blighted core' (19 November 1959).

The twenty-four acres were cleared, but construction did not begin until 1962, after negotiations with the federal and provincial government were finally concluded. Discussions took place around how many of each size of apartment should be built and whether the towers should contain family units or just bachelor and one-bedroom units, with townhouses built in some of the open space. The final product was 900 units in three sixteen-storey wing-shaped towers set in a vast open expanse of grass and parking lots. The base of each tower contained sixteen two-storey units with individual entrances. In the early 1970s a fourth tower was added on the Sherbourne Street frontage.

When council agreed to go ahead with Moss Park, the Alexandra Park scheme to the west of the downtown was put on hold. That scheme proposed to demolish 200 houses on about nine acres of land and to replace them with 380 units in new-style building forms. Residents faced a worrisome future, since council had indicated it wanted to demolish the area – in the southwest quadrant of the Dundas and Spadina intersection – as soon as money was available. The delay meant plans received somewhat more scrutiny, and opposition to clearance began to surface. One letter to the *Globe and Mail* expressed the feelings beginning to emerge about the new-style urban renewal schemes:

I live in Alexandra Park. I own a house here and I live in it and I love it, and so do my six children. It is close to Ryerson, one of the best schools in the city, close to a beautiful new swimming pool. All summer long the children put on their bathing suits at home and walk over for a free swim. On weekends they walk to the Art Gallery or to the harbour or to Old Fort York and sometimes even as far as High Park. These landmarks are a vital part of their everyday life.

Downtown has warm and romantic associations for me and I wanted to be as close to it as possible. That's why I chose to buy a little house near the heart of the city, instead of way off in the cold outskirts ...

It makes my blood boil slightly every time I pick up a paper to see that somebody thinks she'll just waltz in here with her bulldozer and blow my whole little system to smithereens.

To me the whole area is beautiful the way the world is beautiful. The back lanes may have their share of debris, but they also have wild flowers growing in the corners. Some of the front yards are so carefully and lovingly tended that they are still bursting with flowers even now in November. All summer long people of all nationalities sit outdoors and enjoy the everchanging crowded, pushing, pulsing, life of the streets.

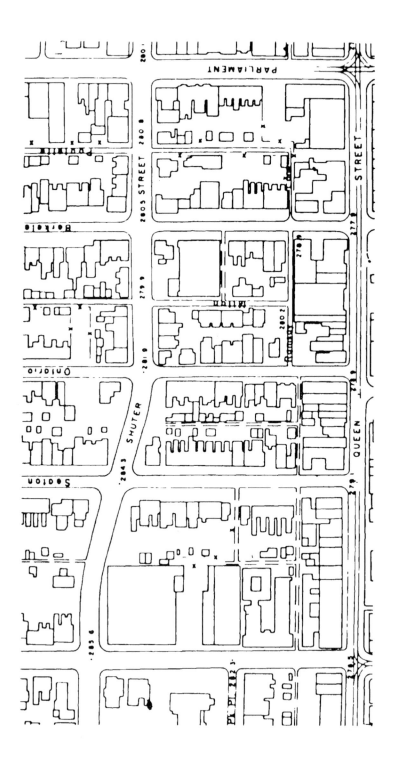

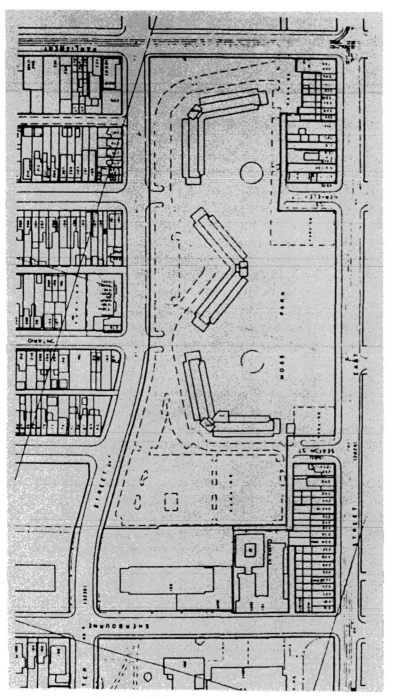

Moss Park, then and now. The continuous open street system has been replaced with a large swath of green space surrounding the three sixteen-storey apartment towers. City of Toronto Planning and Development Department

If the 'experts' want to put up one of these cold, sterile, un-
romantic, low-rental housing projects – which I would hate to even
have within sight of my front door – let them go buy some cheap
land on the outskirts of the city and put it there. Just please, please
don't disturb my warm and darling 'slum.'

(Mrs.) Meg Richardson (21 November 1960)

Mrs Richardson was not to have her way. While there were
several years of discussion about how many units might be
rehabilitated in Alexandra Park, and how many were to be
redeveloped, in 1964 city council made a firm decision to proceed: sixteen acres would be cleared, and 534 new units would
be built. Some 150 units would be renovated.

The new scheme, by architect Jerome Markson, was a more
complicated replay of Regent Park South. The street system was
dispensed with, and in its place was a maze of private walkways
where it was hard to get a sense of which way was north or south.
There was a blurring of common open space and space controlled by the tenant of any particular unit, making everything
outside the front door a kind of no-man's-land. In some cases
walkways ran immediately beside kitchen and living-room windows, giving residents the sense that their privacy was being
invaded by prying eyes of those passing by. Parking was in
common lots that were difficult to police.

The Alexandra Park scheme was approved and implemented,
albeit slowly. By 1966 only twelve new units had been constructed, but City Hall rolled ahead and looked to its next
urban renewal project, Don Mount.

Don Mount was located to the east of Regent Park South,
immediately across the Don River. It fit the urban renewal
stereotype: a mixture of later nineteenth-century residential
and industrial structures that showed signs of neglect. But the
sense of community was strong, and many owners had worked
long and hard at blue-collar jobs to buy their homes. These
owners often complained about the way some absentee owners
kept their properties in a state of disrepair, and how they
failed to take responsibility for the tenants who lived there.

Those complaints didn't create positive concern at City Hall, however, where officials seemed intent on clearing the old away and making a new start.

Don Mount had the feeling of a real community about it. Streets were lined with narrow two- and three-storey townhouses with small and often pleasant front yards. Mature trees overhung the roadways and back lanes. Corner stores provided good local service and places for neighbours to brush shoulders in an informal way.

The city's plan was to replace this community with one entirely different. Roads would be eliminated as would the idea of private yards and private homes. Owners would be expropriated and forced to leave. Tenants had to forage on their own, although city staff were there to look for inexpensive units in other parts of the city. Most often, tenants who lived in Don Mount found the least expensive accommodation was located in the next urban renewal area, then thought to be Trefann Court, south of Regent Park South. Alexandra Park tenants had been through the same experience, which was why some now lived in Don Mount.

In this case, the opposition that had emerged but never crystallized in Alexandra Park found more fertile ground. Represented by member of the Legislative Assembly, James Renwick, and organized by community workers based in Trefann Court, owners in the community came together on the issue of compensation. They wanted fair value for their businesses and for their homes. Existing legislation required expropriating authorities to pay no more than market value for property forcibly taken, and in the case of Don Mount, where values had been depressed by years of talk about urban renewal, that meant homeowners could expect to receive about two-thirds of what was needed to buy a comparable property a few blocks away.

The community engaged in a number of well-publicized demonstrations that raised the whole issue of expropriation and urban renewal at City Hall. Attempts to address City Hall meetings were greeted with hostility from politicians but with more favourable attention from the courts. In the end,

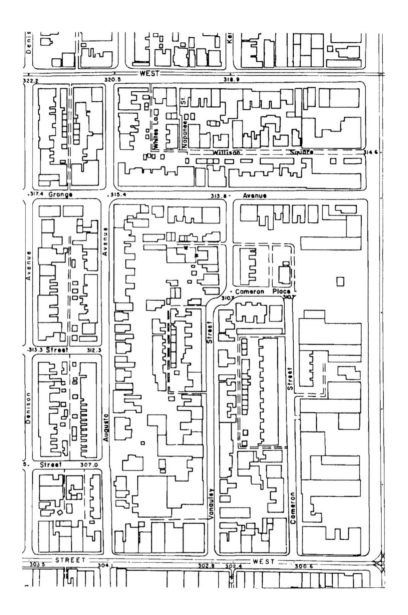

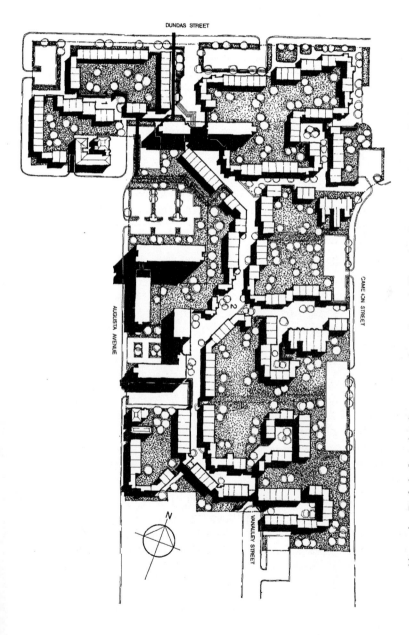

Alexandra Park, before development and as planned. Vanauley Street, running north through the centre of the site, has been reduced to a small stub just north of Queen Street; Grange Avenue, running east/west, has been chopped in two. Even Augusta Avenue has been chopped off before reaching Dundas Street. The new structures are placed in a field without streets. City of Toronto Planning and Development Department

expropriation law was amended by the provincial government to require authorities to hold a hearing of necessity prior to completing any expropriation, and to pay compensation substantial enough to permit acquisition of a comparable replacement property in the city (Sewell 1972, 27ff).

The victory with the expropriation legislation came too late to save Don Mount. In spite of several court battles to prevent the city from evicting residents and gaining physical possession of properties, by the time the Expropriation Act had been amended most of the homes had been demolished, the roads had been closed, and construction had begun on the new public housing project. Like Alexandra Park, the new Don Mount project was designed by a leading Toronto architect (in this case Raymond Moriyama, although he divorced himself from its ultimate implementation) with disregard, perhaps even contempt, for the history of how this land had previously been planned. The project consisted of 250 stacked townhouses around several courtyards, with parking lots separating housing units from abutting streets, severing any relationship the new community might have with the surrounding neighbourhood and its rows of nineteenth-century homes.

The fight about Don Mount did not raise questions of urban design directly, as had begun to surface in Alexandra Park; however, it did question the effects of urban renewal on older parts of the city. Those questions were thrown into stark focus when city council began to implement plans for the next urban renewal area, Trefann Court.

Trefann Court is an area immediately south of Regent Park South, bounded by Parliament, Shuter, River, and Queen streets. Most of the area was occupied by traditional nineteenth-century row housing, interrupted here and there by industrial plants, with corner stores, retail shops on Queen Street near Parliament Street, and a large new five-storey industrial building at Sumach Street. Eugene Faludi prepared a plan for Toronto Industrial Leaseholds Co. Ltd, the owner of the new industrial building, in 1956: that plan and the subsequent city-sponsored urban renewal plans called for the demolition of all residential buildings and the retention of the new industrial structure.

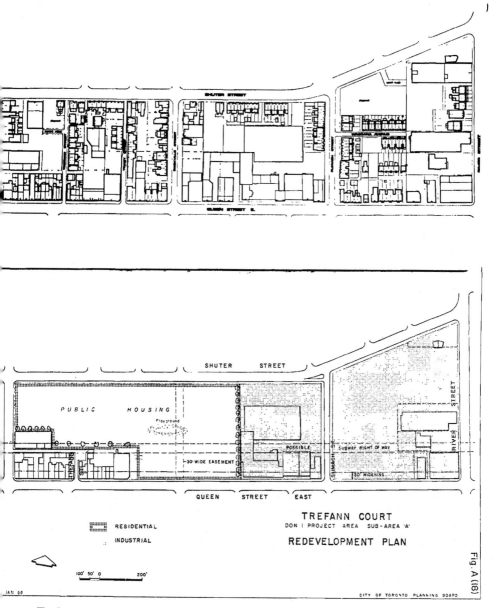

Trefann Court, 1966. The top shows the land uses as they were in 1966; the bottom shows the Redevelopment Plan. Apart from a few retail outlets at Queen and Parliament streets, the whole area would be demolished so a fresh start could be made. The street system is to be replaced by superblocks.

City of Toronto Planning Board

The western half of the site would be used for new residential units in the modern vein; the eastern half would be sold off for industrial purposes.

When plans were revealed in 1966 – they had been rumoured for almost twenty years – residents began to object mightily. As an alternative to demolition, they urged rehabilitation, perhaps also as a way of escaping the perils of the expropriation law, which had yet to be amended. Many deputations were made to City Hall, and the mayor of the day, Philip Givens, retorted with the then current approach to change in downtown neighbourhoods: 'You have to break eggs to make an omelette.'

Givens and his staff were not to get their way. After four years of demonstrations, Trefann residents found their own elected voices in City Hall in 1970, and city council soon decided that any plans for the area had to be drawn up in consultation with local residents and businessmen. This was done, and a plan sympathetic to local interests was adopted and implemented. (The Trefann Court fight is described in much more detail in Sewell, 1972, chapter 2, and Fraser 1972.)

Trefann brought about three significant changes to planning in Toronto. First, it was agreed that the old urban renewal plans would be abandoned and that a working committee of local residents and businessmen would have responsibility for developing new plans. The idea that ordinary people could be involved in city planning was a major blow to the new suburbanist approach, which relied on experimentation, total clearance, and the mysticism of the private planner. Those principles were replaced by a much more mundane approach that relied on local experience and desires.

Second, residents demanded, and obtained, the right to select the planner who would work with them in developing the new plan. When residents first asked that the planner be located in a nearby office to be accessible, they were told by city officials that the constant consultation implied by such accessibility would interfere with planning 'professionalism' and independence. Under pressure the politicians backed down, eventually agreeing not only to a local planning office but also that residents could be involved in staff selection. Residents were pleased

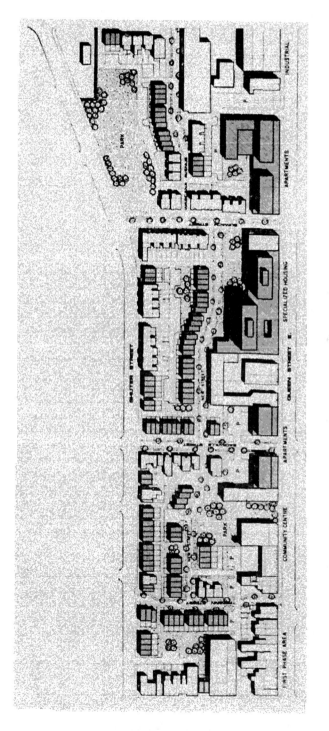

The Trefann Court plan, 1972. The residents' plan recommended by the Trefann Court Working Committee of local residents, with the guidance of planner Howard Cohen, was finally adopted by council. It proceeds on the simple assumption that existing streets should be retained and new streets opened. Fraser 1972

with the idea they could have a more direct say in planning decisions about their neighbourhood, and participation quickly spread. Both planners and architects were forced to show what would work and why, in the process setting aside the fancy and often unsupportable theories that led to places such as Flemingdon Park.

In this way planning became less an exercise in vision and adherence to theory, and more an opportunity to implement things that seemed to work, regardless of what planners thought of them. This approach became known under one of two rubrics: 'citizen participation' to those who were more interested in process; or 'neighbourhood protection' for those more interested in product.

Third, the nature of the resulting plan was radically different from that produced by planners working on their own. The plan developed by the working committee and eventually adopted by city council and the various levels of government was ordinary in every sense of the word: it strengthened and extended the existing street system, and it encouraged new housing on empty lots or to replace structures in very poor condition, housing that had front and back yards, and buildings that faced directly onto public streets. The new found its place among the old rather than trying to obliterate or displace it.

Trefann Court spelled the end of urban renewal in Canada. The political turmoil generated by it and comparable schemes in Halifax and Vancouver led the federal government to establish, in 1968, a task force to review housing policy. The task force was headed by cabinet minister Paul Hellyer, a former residential developer from Toronto. The task force suggested housing questions were best left to the private sector, and recommended that the federal government stop being a direct player in housing, instead limiting its role to support for the private sector. It was highly critical of the whole approach to urban renewal and recommended significant change, in effect suggesting the solution might be worse than the disease.

The Hellyer task force signalled a major change for the federal government: the use of government as the implementer of the modern planning vision through urban renewal was at an end. The government slowly moved to programs that stressed neighbourhood rehabilitation. In the years before the task force, however, the new planning ideas found support in schemes proposed by the private sector. Government-sponsored schemes such as Regent Park and Moss Park were followed by private-sector projects that cleared large numbers of houses, replacing them with high-rise apartment buildings.

Foremost of these schemes was St Jamestown, a superblock of sixteen apartment buildings on the edge of downtown Toronto. Agents operating for a development consortium called the Parliament Street Syndicate began assembling homes in the area bounded by Parliament, Wellesley, Sherbourne, and Bloor streets in the mid 1950s. Preparing for the coming of the high-rise apartment tower, Toronto City Council had in 1953 zoned this superblock and other areas on the edge of the downtown up to a density of 3.5, thus permitting 3.5 square feet of floor space for every square foot of land. Since areas of houses around the downtown were generally zoned at less than one times coverage, permitting little change, this new designation was very provocative, opening many areas up to significant change.

The St Jamestown area consisted of comfortable two- and three-storey homes built in the 1870s for the upper middle class. The syndicate hired the W.W. Gardiner Real Estate Company – headed by the son of Metro chairman Fred Gardiner – to assemble these homes, and by the middle of 1956 more than half the 435 properties were purchased or under option. The syndicate approached city council with the suggestion it should expropriate on behalf of the development, but that was rejected as a poor precedent for the use of city powers. As well, the development proposal was put on hold, since the developer did not own all the property (Fox and Winton 1979).

The beginning of the land assembly sealed the fate of the community, however. With such a high proportion of homes controlled by developers whose intention was demolition, incentives for repair quickly disappeared and properties fell into poor condition – in turn confirming the belief that change would come sooner rather than later. Two high-rise towers –

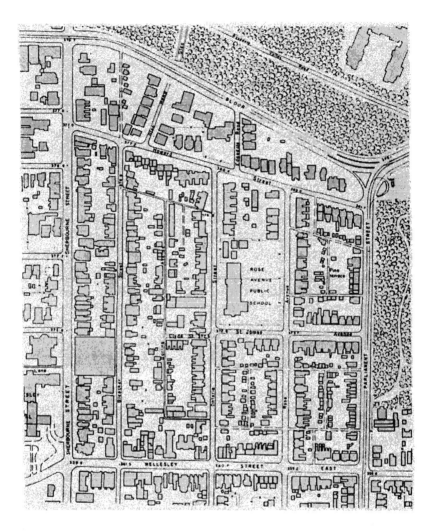

St Jamestown before and after development. The first sketch shows the neighbourhood before development in the 1960s; the second shows how, by the 1980s, the plan first conceived for the Parliament Street Syndicate had been implemented, closing most streets, building tall slab apartment towers, and leaving most of the space covered in grass or asphalt. City of Toronto Planning and Development Department

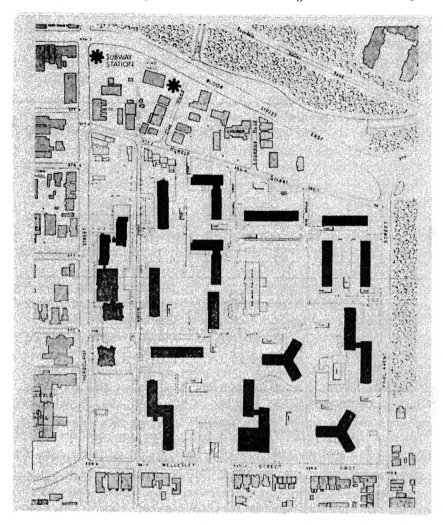

the Barbara Apartments at 700 and 730 Ontario Street – were built with Central Mortgage and Housing Corporation funding in 1959 in the middle of the superblock. The syndicate collapsed, but other investors entered the picture, including Shabse Frankel from New York, Belmont Construction, Meridian Development, and the Rose Park Group. Over the next few years, housing was demolished and replaced by high-rise towers set in green grass and surface parking lots. By the middle of the 1960s city council had agreed to rezonings for development schemes covering all of the superblock over to Bleecker Street.

Block-busting – a deliberate tactic used by developers to run down properties they controlled, forcing holdout owners to consider selling as quickly as possible – made redevelopment seem inevitable. A developer would purchase a property, then lease it to a middleman to run in the short term. The middleman would lease to the most downtrodden of tenants, usually roomers whose lives had fallen apart. The house would quickly become unkept: repairs would not be made, walks would not be shovelled in winter, and garbage accumulated on porches and lawns. The occupants of the house often had severe alcohol problems, and parties would end in shouting, fighting, and men lying in back lanes. Fire was a constant fear and a frequent occurrence. Several such houses on any one block could significantly alter the character of the neighbourhood.

Nearby owners not only had to put up with these changes – both middlemen and developers disclaimed responsibility, while city officials said they were powerless to intervene – but found that fire insurance companies refused to renew contracts, putting owners at considerable risk. At this point owners decided it was time to move. Since likely purchasers did not find the area attractive, the only offer they could expect would be from the developer who had caused the problems in the first place. Hence developers quickly gained a stranglehold on a residential neighbourhood they wished to assemble. (For a more extensive description of block-busting techniques see Sewell 1972, chapter 8.)

The end result was that owners in St Jamestown contented

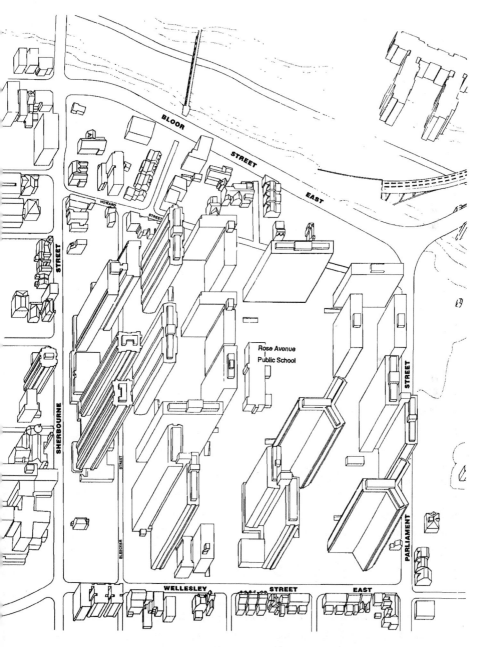

·ST. JAMES TOWN REVITALIZATION·

St Jamestown now, isometric. The overwhelming scale of the new contrasts with the old – the three-storey structures on the south side of Wellesley Street, at the bottom of the sketch, look very puny indeed. City of Toronto Planning and Development Department

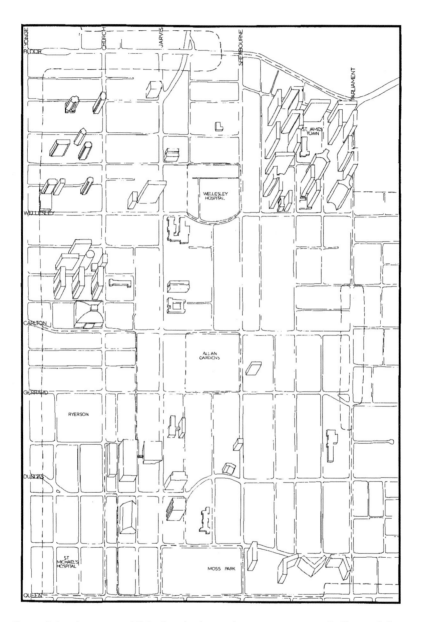

East of the downtown. This sketch shows the new structures built as of the mid 1970s in accordance with the official plan approved by council in 1969 – the remainder of the area was occupied by two- and three-storey structures.

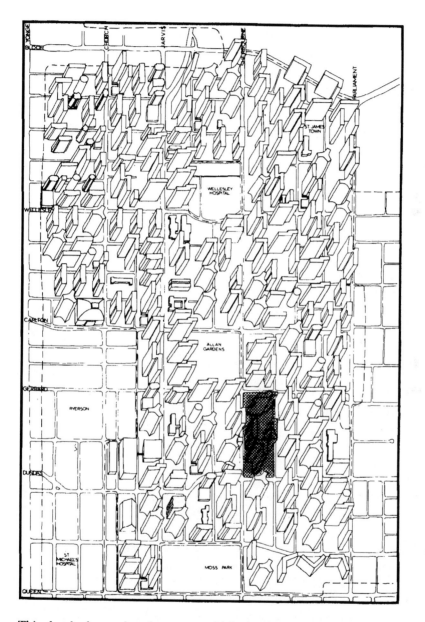

This sketch shows what the area would look like if the city's official plan were fully implemented. The shaded area became the Dundas/Sherbourne project discussed in the next chapter. The only area that was fully built is St Jamestown, indistinguishable from what was planned for the whole precinct. It is the top right superblock, just to the right of Wellesley Hospital.
Diamond and Myers

themselves with getting the most money they could for their properties. As for the proposed apartment tower plans, they were warmly welcomed by Walter Manthorpe, who had joined city planning staff in the mid 1950s and in 1962 was appointed commissioner of development, with the specific task of aiding developers in their assemblies and rezonings.

Manthorpe had gained his development experience in London, rebuilding bombed-out areas in the modern style. 'I was the guy who set up the standards which allowed high buildings to exist in London,' he said. 'I had designed the site planning standards for the buildings to be built after the war. It involved the concept of angular planes: vertical and horizontal. The result is buildings being set back on the site, going higher. These things are now embodied in the zoning bylaw; I took my London experience, which was not in bylaw form, and rewrote the relevant bylaw.' (Powell 1972, 107–8) For these obvious reasons, Manthorpe was a strong supporter of the plan for St Jamestown – tall, thin buildings set in a sea of grass. Indeed, by the early 1970s, Manthorpe had resigned as commissioner of development and was taken on by the Meridian Group, one of the key developers. St Jamestown was built much as conceived by the Parliament Street Syndicate, but by a number of different developers rather than by one company.

This style of development – tower in the park – was one favoured by developers and city planners alike. While St Jamestown was Toronto's largest single collection of this new planning model that Le Corbusier had drawn in the early 1930s (see chapter 1), other examples abounded. There were instances of single new towers in many locations to the east of downtown and one large area of such structures just north of High Park, where again developers slowly acquired houses, demolished them, and obtained city permission to build new towers surrounded by grass. Likely sites were chosen along the Bloor/Danforth subway line, which opened in the early 1960s, assemblies begun, and rezoning applications made.

But these new apartment towers were not readily accepted by local residents. Objections were made to the contrast in scale between what remained and what was proposed; to the kind of housing provided, which seemed inappropriate to families; and to the massive change these towers created in the sense of community and neighbourhood. Across Toronto, harassed groups of residents met to work out strategies that would contain this new style of city building. Their opposition was not so much to change as to wholesale displacement, the rejection of the old and its replacement with a new that seemed to insult what had been demolished.

There clearly was a demand for this new housing, one created by baby-boomers born just after the Second World War who wanted a place of their own to live in as soon as they began working. That demand fuelled the fires of the development industry, which responded with plans for many large towers surrounded by grass. But the developers found themselves pitted against residents' groups, and that struggle found some resolution at City Hall, where elections in 1969 and 1972 brought fresh voices to express the sentiments of those opposed to the new ways of planning.

6

Creating
an Alternative
to Modernism

Modern planning spawned its own opposition. The burgeoning new suburbs led not to a decrease in housing prices but to an increase, and many young professionals decided to reject the suburban alternative and live instead in old houses downtown smack in the way of the expressways planned to serve the new communities on the fringes of the city. Together with those who had been involved in saving Old City Hall, and those trying to protect neighbourhoods from urban renewal and private redevelopment, the expressway fighters created a potent political force that elected a reform city council in Toronto in 1972.

The new council lost no time in re-writing the planning rules that had been adopted less than two decades before. A strategy was set leading to a new plan for the downtown – one that discouraged single-use office buildings in windy plazas – and alternatives to tower-in-the-park apartment buildings in residential neighbourhoods. The new order at City Hall sponsored its own initiates, buying forty-five acres on the edge of downtown to plan and build the radically traditional St Lawrence Community, and proposing housing developments based on alternative planning principles in many neighbourhoods. By the mid 1970s, it was clear that the modernist approach had few friends or allies in the city itself.

Ironically, it was the success of suburbs like Don Mills that ultimately created the movement signalling the decline of modern planning ideas in the city. Since 1952, variants on the Don Mills style had crowded the edge of the city, more than doubling the developed size of the urban area in a brief twenty years. But suburban house costs didn't decrease; they increased. Families purchased in the suburbs for a variety of reasons – cost, housing space, prestige. It is not fair to assume they moved there to endorse a particular planning style or approach. As S.D. Clark noted: 'People moved out to the suburbs in search of space. They wanted a house, and the only place they could find a house was in the suburbs. What views people had about suburban living had little to do with their becoming suburbanites. If there was a selection, it was one largely of a negative character' (Clark 1966, 223).

For many, buying a new house was a *sine qua non* of success, and new houses were only found in the suburbs, which was one reason the market for them was so strong. Suburban neighbourhoods designed by Faludi and Hancock were meant for the middle class – that was why high design standards were imposed, and why such care was taken to ensure a homogeneous population of owners. But as land was assembled in large chunks, and as demand outpaced supply, developers were able to substantially increase asking prices for building lots. House prices, fuelled by the large number of new suburban homes for sale, rose quickly in the early 1960s, much more quickly than incomes.

Prices showed a gradual increase throughout the 1950s and then, in the early 1960s, as suburban construction began to dominate the market, the explosion occurred. Average prices of homes sold through the Toronto Real Estate Board – accounting for almost all sales – rose from $14,400 in 1953 to $16,500 by 1963, but then rose sharply, reaching $19,000 by 1965 and $24,600 by 1967, and continuing their upward climb (Pendergrast 1981, 131). From the incomplete data available, it is clear that new (suburban) homes were sold at prices considerably above average multiple listing sales, and thus far above prices obtained by older homes in the central city. The average cost of a new home in 1963 was $20,811; total multiple listing service (MLS) sales, including new homes, was only $16,517, indicating that the cost of a 'used' house must have been less than $15,000. As the decade continued, the difference between the two increased. In the later 1960s the cost of an older resale house in the developed part of the city was 35 to 40 per cent less than a new suburban house (Pendergrast 1981, 125). The cost of a new suburban house in Toronto rose from twice the average family income in 1953 to three times the average family income in 1971 (Sewell 1992).

Young, upwardly mobile, middle-class couples looking to purchase homes were obviously aware of the difference in price between what was offered new in the suburbs and used in the city. The more adventurous thought of buying downtown, although it was not seen as a widely desirable choice: the house wouldn't be new; the neighbourhood wouldn't be homogenous, and more likely than not the young professionals would be better educated than anyone else on the street; and of course it wasn't fashionable. Others, wishing to signal early disillusionment with North American social values (a split that broke wide open with the war in Vietnam), would favour downtown as a positive choice.

Architect Irving Grossman, himself designing suburban neighbourhoods such as Edgeley Village in the Jane/Finch corridor of North York, purchased sixteen houses on Alpha Avenue in the Parliament/Wellesley areas in the mid 1960s (the name Cabbagetown was only extended to this part of Toronto in the 1970s) and undertook extensive renovations. To make the houses appear fresh after one hundred years of city life, Grossman painted them white, both inside and out. The houses were rented or sold to young professionals, some of whom had previously lived in European cities as students (Lorimer 1971).

The pattern was followed on adjacent streets in the next few years, and 'white-painting' was widespread. University professors and other professionals made the same kinds of changes to the larger homes in the Annex, just north of the University of Toronto, although this area was closer to the respectable areas of Rosedale and Forest Hill. Here, the physical changes required, particularly white-painting, were not seen as quite so necessary.

Style was important to this process. White-painting made old homes feel new, and a coat of white paint on the exterior – in contrast with neighbouring homes clad in dirty brick or the traditional brick red paint – signalled to others the change that was coming. As enough 'urban adventurers' (as the Toronto *Star* called them) established a beach-head in the area, the importance of white-painting faded. Instead, owners cleaned brick by sand-blasting or, when the damage of sand-blasting became clear, with chemicals.

The effect of this movement, driven by higher prices in new suburban housing and lower prices in downtown housing, was to infuse the downtown with a host of young professionals who

were not intimidated by their counterparts in government bu-
reaucracies. In most American cities as the middle class fled to
the suburbs, the disparity of experience and talent between
government officials and remaining downtown residents grew:
in Toronto, that disparity narrowed as the young professionals
moved in. Now there was much less reticence among downtown
residents to question change.

Hence it was the new suburbs helped to fuel the debate
about the future of the city. Questions of urban design and
structure, which planners had previously been able to resolve
by themselves with a relatively free hand, constricted only by a
development industry concerned more with profits than the
niceties of planning theory, now became fraught with difficulty
and divided opinion. The new residents weren't eager to accept
the word of other professionals at face value.

This change was most evident in the struggle around transportation. The self-contained assumption of Don Mills was not
fulfilled – fewer than 5 per cent of residents worked there, even
though plans had called for half the residents to work within
the community – and its progeny, which was much less carefully
planned, did not even reach that small percentage. Residents
in the new suburbs expected to work downtown, where the
high-paying jobs were located, and they needed some fast means
of transportation. The preferred mode was the expressway.

Toronto's first urban expressway ran up the Don Valley to
Don Mills and beyond. At its initial meeting in 1953, the new
Metro Council had asked the provincial government to build
this roadway, connecting the downtown with the new Highway
401 bypass to the north, and the road had been built. It was
followed later that decade by the Gardiner Expressway, built
alongside the railway tracks close to the lake. Neither expressway
raised significant opposition.

Metro transportation planners, aware of the likelihood of
burgeoning suburban growth, prepared a scheme to lace the
urban area with expressways, including three more radiating
out from the city centre – the Highway 400 extension, the
Spadina, and Scarborough – and the Crosstown, which would
provide an inner link between a number of those super-high-

ways. The roadways fit the new planning philosophy perfectly, since they called for remaking the city in a radical fashion, starting with wholesale demolition and ending with the construction of parking lots for the cars that used them, as well as new buildings in the new style. The inner city expressway was the mark of the modern city.

The Spadina Expressway proposed to cut through neighbourhoods to the north and west of the University of Toronto, winding south from Highway 401 through ravines and residential areas, finally ending on Spadina Avenue within shouting distance of the central downtown. It promised demolition of close to one thousand houses, and total disruption of the community patterns in the west central part of the city. It became the focus of the city's most serious fight yet between the modern and the traditional planning visions.

Those who lived in the suburbs had difficulty understanding why anyone would want to save older neighbourhoods, or an urban form that was past its time. Suburbanites thought it entirely reasonable that the existing city be demolished to make way for the new city, including building roadways necessary to join the downtown office towers where people worked to the suburban houses where they lived.

City residents didn't quite see it that way. They argued that their homes were important to them and shouldn't be destroyed; that the cost of the expressway was unreasonable; that the time savings were minuscule; that the downtown would be one giant parking lot; that public transit was a much better investment than roads for more cars. The arguments were put most forcefully in *The Bad Trip*, a book by David and Nadine Nowlan. David Nowlan was a young economics professor at the University of Toronto; Nadine was one of the chief organizers of the anti-expressway coalition, who was elected to Toronto City Council in 1985.

Under the leadership of university professor Alan Powell, who brought students infected with the idealism of the 1960s into the fray, the coalition called itself sssoccc, Stop Spadina Save Our City Co-ordinating Committee. It included not just faculty members of the university and young white-painters, but the cultural and financial elite of the city who felt their own neighbourhoods of Forest Hill and Rosedale would be affected adversely, if not by the Spadina Expressway, then by the Crosstown. The Save Our City name gave due recognition to the character of the fight, which pitted one kind of vision about the city against another, a battle between suburban and city values. Whether they knew it or not, suburbanites appeared to be taking seriously Clarence Stein's call to demolish the existing city.

sssoccc organized a powerful lobby, taking every advantage of the willingness to demonstrate, crowd political meetings, investigate ties and links among various politicians, and respond to every scintilla of support evidenced for the expressway. For their part, proponents of the Spadina did the same, and political lines were more toughly drawn than the city had seen for many decades. The line seemed to run between supporters of the old city and the new.

The fight over the expressway erupted both at Toronto City Council and then at Metro Council, in the last few years of the decade. sssoccc did its homework until a majority of city council opposed the expressway, but the suburban politicians on Metro Council, augmented by city members believing in 'progress,' ensured that Metro Council, as instigator and partial funder of the road, continued in favour. The issue found its way into the municipal election in 1969, and several of those elected to Toronto City Council – William Kilbourn, Karl Jaffary, Ying Hope, and John Sewell – made it clear they were going to continue the fight at City and Metro councils, and if necessary at the provincial level where funds were still required to be committed before Metro could begin construction. Where local politicians stood on the Spadina Expressway was the defining issue of the day. Two opposing visions of the city had rarely been presented in such a powerful, volatile, and bitter way.

In June 1971, after four years of almost nonstop demonstrations and strategy sessions, the anti-expressway forces triumphed. William Davis, newly appointed head of Ontario's Conservative government, announced in the Legislative Assembly: 'If we are building a transportation system to serve the automobile, the Spadina Expressway would be a good place to start. But if we are building a transportation system to serve people, the Spadina Expressway is a good place to stop.'

Dennis Lee celebrated the victory with a poem:

Sparrows sniffed the air, and hung
Like humming-birds with bubblegum
Doing pushups in the sun
   The day we stopped Spadina.

I watched the people touch the air
And feel the green renewal there
As though a headline was a prayer
   The day we stopped Spadina.

I saw a woman's face which glowed
I saw computer cards explode
And I heard grass grow on Walmer Road
   The day we stopped Spadina.

And Bishop Strachan from underground
Was half converted by the sound
Of pleasure in Toronto town
   The day we stopped Spadina.

I don't have a dollar, I don't have a dime
And the waiter keeps saying it's past closing time
And sometimes this city is no friend of mine
   And if I can't get cinzano I'll go back on wine
And sometimes my own life is no friend of mine
But none of that matters when I call to mind
   The one and only day we stopped Spadina.
    (Powell 1972, 114)

Although no one was quite sure if the beast was really dead – Jane Jacobs claimed expressways were like dragons, with numerous lives – city residents who had participated in the struggle had a chance to celebrate and catch their breath: the city had not been totally overrun. The expressway was never brought back to life, in spite of numerous attempts over the next fifteen years by suburban politicians to try slight reroutings and other ploys.

The anti-expressway crowd was one of four groupings of people struggling against the new planning values in the city. The other three groups were mentioned in chapter 5: those trying to protect the city's older buildings from destruction by large downtown projects; residents pushing to protect their neighbourhoods from the ravages of urban renewal; and residents fighting rezonings for apartment towers that didn't fit in their neighbourhoods.

Only in a peripheral sense did the groups feel they were fighting for the same cause, and thus the struggles emerged and flowered independently, calling on a wide and diverse variety of people. The common link was generally provided by the politicians: in almost every case residents involved in each issue found those who voted for their interests were the same four or five councillors voting for the interests of those involved in the other issues; and those who opposed them were the remaining eighteen or nineteen council members. In 1971 and 1972 individuals in each of the four interests realized they shared much in common, and various kinds of overlap occurred, producing a rough reform grouping in the city. The grouping was based on who supported what: it meant that those involved in fighting urban renewal schemes could acknowledge that plans for Metro Centre probably weren't worth supporting, without having to understand the intricacies of the land transactions or the density controls; and those fighting high-rise apartments could also oppose urban renewal without wondering whether Trefann Court really was a slum that should be destroyed.

A loose coalition under the name Community Organizing 1972 (co72) came together to provoke likely candidates to run, and then give them encouragement, in the December 1972 municipal election. The group consisted of community activists, three of the reform-minded alderman elected in 1969 – Bill Kilbourn, Karl Jaffary, and John Sewell – and representatives from the Metro Toronto Labour Council. While that coalition was successful in convincing independent candidates to run in a number of wards, it never produced a manifesto, an agenda, or a statement of principles. Instead, the ideas holding people together were rough and undigested – that expressways should be opposed; that people should be involved in planning decisions; that development was not an unsullied good; and that neighbourhoods should be protected from high-rise development. The agreement was more on the specifics of issues being discussed than on the underlying principles that threaded people together.

Thus the reform agenda was never reduced to a single statement. Reform sentiment, however, was broad enough to pervade the election, and reformers captured eleven of the twenty-three council seats. David Crombie, who had been elected in 1969 as alderman but had not taken an active part in many of the tough reform votes and actions of those working with CO72, had unexpectedly announced his candidacy as mayor four months before the December 1972 election. With his brilliant talent for simplifying difficult issues and giving them a friendly edge, Crombie gave city-wide voice to ideas such as protecting neighbourhoods and resident participation in planning, and was also elected. While Crombie as alderman had not been seen to commit himself whole-heartedly to the reform cause, for the next several years as mayor he found himself entangled within the popularity that came with being characterized as a reformer. More often than not, he implemented the reform agenda (Caulfield 1974).

With Crombie's support, there was a slim working reform majority on city council. That permitted council to begin making the changes necessary to stop the spread of modernist planning ideas. One of the first concerns lay in the link between transportation and land use – the prime example of which had been the Spadina Expressway. Early in 1973, council established the Core Area Task Force in response to a Metro proposal to create a one-way street system in downtown Toronto. The task force consisted of a wide range of community activists and, under the leadership of Alderman Colin Vaughan, quickly assumed effective jurisdiction over planning matters in the whole central area of the city. It quickly spun off studies on housing, office space projections, and nonresidential open space.

The task force gave voice to an alternative agenda for the downtown, one that saw new construction fitting with the existing city rather than destroying it or pushing it aside. In its report issued in 1974, for instance, it talked about new approaches to housing:

New housing can be constructed on existing vacant lots. But this must be done on a scale that is consistent with existing housing and in line with other housing so that the streetscape is not destroyed ...

The City's Zoning and Building bylaws, which now have certain setbacks and other requirements that prevent infilling, should be amended to allow infilling where [planning] studies show this would be desirable. (Core Area Task Force 1974, 157)

The task force also sponsored the publication *On Building Downtown* in 1974. The report was prepared for the City Planning Department by architect George Baird, who proposed new design guidelines for the downtown. Baird looked at the downtown in terms of public amenities, and questioned whether discrete projects designed without regard for surrounding spaces and structures – characteristics that seemed to be a hallmark of the new planning – produced a desirable city. He suggested the key concern should be placing new buildings in appropriate contexts, and that changed planning controls would be necessary:

The present system of zoning is not adequate. Zoning regulates use, size, and density, and to a certain extent, setbacks and envelopes. It is a concept related to definable, isolated parcels of land, not to the more important issues – the relatedness of these parcels – and their connections and their impacts on neighbouring lands. The current set of rigid controls forces the participants in the development process into a reactive position. The experiments since 1963 in 'bonusing' have been attempts to encourage public amenity through an unrelated incentive of increased density ... We also appreciate the inability of zoning to address itself to connections and impact. The need for re-appraisal is evident. (Baird 1974, 5)

The way Baird addressed questions of interrelatedness was by looking at qualities such as sun and shade, wind and calm, noise and quietude, public views, linkages between the public and private realms, historic buildings, and other design issues. He offered a subtle critique of recent planning approaches, using Toronto examples of desirable and undesirable results. His study made a very strong case for designs that fit buildings into the existing city rather than trying to reshape it in a radical fashion. It was couched in practical straightforward language, without resort to planning theory, making it convincing in the political realm. Baird did not argue the merits of open space as a good in and of itself; instead, he cited obvious negative impacts of particular large open spaces and accompanying windy gusts. He rejected banishing retail uses from the street and into the underground, and also the destruction of important buildings from previous eras. This study quickly became the guidebook for developers and planners alike, making developments modeled on the Toronto-Dominion Centre and new City Hall most unlikely.

As the Core Area Task Force was getting established in 1973, council considered and ultimately passed a holding bylaw that restricted the approval of large buildings while the official plan for the central area was being rethought. Known as the '45 Foot Bylaw,' this instrument permitted only new buildings under forty-five feet high and less than 40,000 square feet in floor area to be built during the two or three years when the new plan was being formulated. It was strongly criticized by the development industry, but supported even more strongly by resident groups. The room for reconsideration created by this bylaw meant that the ascendant reform ideas could be reduced to specifics in the new plan for the downtown. After much debate, some of it acrimonious since some council members felt the recommended action didn't go far enough, the Central Area Plan was passed by council in 1976.

The plan made substantial amendments reducing the amount of office space permitted in the downtown, tying the provision of new office space to the capacity of the transportation system to carry more office workers in and out of the downtown, as recommended by the Core Area Task Force. It went further, and implemented policies at considerable variance to modernist planning theory. Segregated uses in the downtown were henceforth discouraged: housing should be built in the midst of office areas to ensure a vibrant urban environment. Contrary to the theory underlying the Toronto-Dominion Centre, retail uses would be encouraged and even required at grade. Large open plazas would be prohibited. Historic buildings would be preserved by zoning tricks such as density bonuses. There were strong disagreements about the plan among councillors, with the tougher reformers arguing that permitted densities were too high and that the encouragement of affordable housing was not strong enough. But there was wide consensus rejecting the modernist planning ideology.

Substantial changes were also made to the bylaws controlling housing form. Densities would henceforth be calculated by units per acre rather than the floor-space index: the old measurement produced small apartments to maximize the number of rentable units, an unfair restriction, it was thought, when there was a need downtown for larger units suitable for either families or higher-income tenants. Encouragement would be given to grade-related units – a recognition that unless clear instructions were given, such units may not be offered in high-density developments. Permissable residential densities were increased significantly so developers could consider housing an economic option on expensive downtown land, and in several districts maximum densities could only be obtained if residential uses were combined with commercial, in a mixed-use structure.

Contemporaneous with council's move to implement the new ideas in the Central Area Plan, attempts were made to unravel planning approvals already given for projects in the modernist style. A long-drawn-out redevelopment struggle was in its final stages at the northeast corner of Dundas and

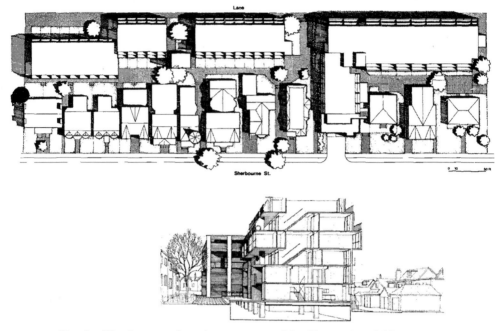

Dundas/Sherbourne, the scheme proposed by Diamond and Myers, 1971. Only one structure on Sherbourne Street is proposed for demolition, allowing the five- and six-storey apartment building a sizable access to the street. The house-form buildings dating from as early as 1845 remain. Most of the new building fronts a wide laneway, and a walkway divides the old and the new structures. A.J. Diamond

Dundas/Sherbourne, photo of a portion of the development as built. A.J. Diamond

Sherbourne streets, where a developer proposed to demolish thirty large homes built in the ninteenth century – indeed, the block contained housing built in every decade between 1840 and 1910 – and replace it with two twenty-eight-storey towers surrounded by spacious grassy lawns. The development concept had been approved by city council in 1970, but local residents and the heritage group Time and Place appealed the matter to the Ontario Municipal Board in 1972. During the hearing a new plan was produced by the innovative architectural firm Diamond and Myers. This plan proposed as many units as the proposed towers, but it retained and renovated most of the old buildings, constructing a six-storey apartment block at the rear. It was advanced as a good example of how redevelopment could fit in with and strengthen an existing neighbourhood. The OMB was obviously impressed, and threw out the rezoning for the two tall towers.

Early in 1973, with the new Reform Council just esconsed in office, the developer decided to tear down some of the old buildings, starting with a house built in 1845 by Enoch Turner, a brewer who had given Toronto its first free school. Demonstrations ensued and, as a last hope to prevent destruction of existing buildings, city council was dragooned into purchasing the site. As it turned out, this was the first project of the city's fledging nonprofit housing company, CityHome, which was incorporated in 1974, and the city ultimately built the Diamond and Myers plan (Caulfield 1974, 46–8).

At the same time, council struggled with whether it should repeal other bylaws passed by the previous council permitting high-rise apartment projects in neighbourhoods. Mayor Crombie thought repealing bylaws was an abrogation of the process, but he was unable to convince a majority of council of his position and, eventually, bylaws for two contentious projects were repealed.

For the Quebec/Gothic development near High Park in the city's west end, in 1971 city council had approved the destruction of about one hundred houses on two streets and the construction of three large apartment towers. In 1973, after much negotiation, a new scheme was agreed to which retained

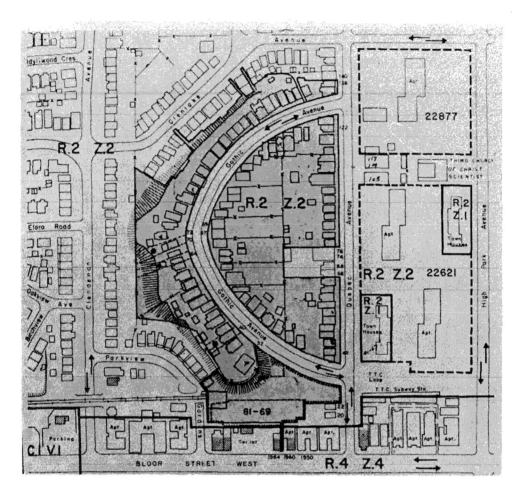

Quebec/Gothic site. The reason for the name of the arched street is clear in this plan. The site outlined in grey is the land assembled by the developer – the last area of homes left from a larger neighbourhood to the east has already been replaced with apartments set in grass. The letters R2 Z2 are a city zoning designation; the numbers with five digits indicate special rezoning bylaws for the sites within dotted lines. City of Toronto Planning and Development Department

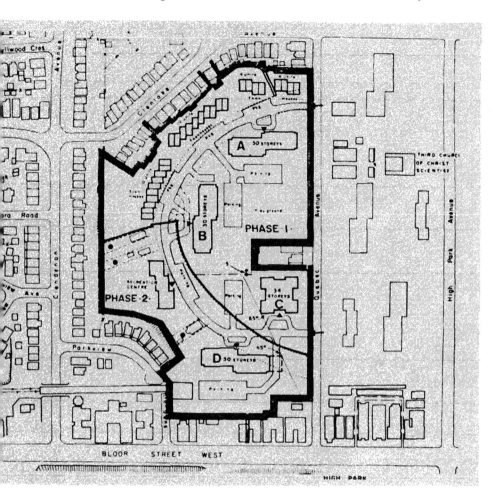

Quebec/Gothic proposed development, 1971. All houses within the assembly west of Quebec Avenue would be demolished, to be replaced by four apartment buildings, a recreation centre, and a number of townhouses. City of Toronto Planning and Development Department

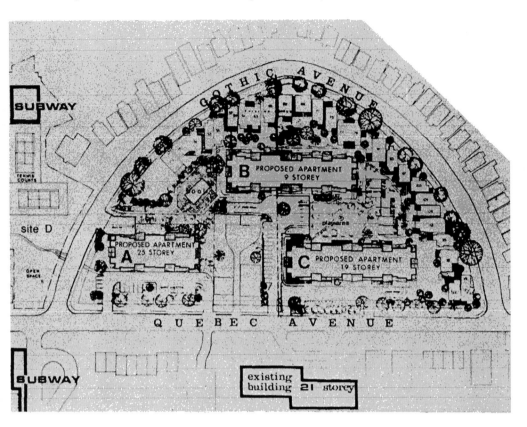

Quebec/Gothic negotiated scheme. This scheme, worked out between the developer and local residents in 1974 after pressure from city council, retains all houses on the west side of Gothic and most of those on the east side. The tradeoff demanded by the developer was three apartment buildings, but they are incorporated in a way that does not overshadow the existing community.
City of Toronto Planning and Development Department

all but a handful of the homes that were to have been destroyed, incorporating into the fabric of the existing community several apartment buildings.

In the case of an assembly on McCaul Street, on the edge of the downtown, council had given planning approval for several large apartment towers: after discussions with the developer, this scheme was replaced by a series of mid-size apartment buildings over retail space in what is now known as Village by the Grange. As with Quebec/Gothic, the resulting development was much kinder and more supportive of the structures and community surrounding the development site. The revised scheme added to the neighbourhood rather than trying to replace it. (For further detail, see Caulfield 1974, chap. 3.)

The epitome of the new planning approach taken by the Reform Council was the development of the St Lawrence community in a derelict industrial area to the south and east of the city's core. This area was originally part of the lake, but it had been filled in during the 1860s as the railway came to Toronto's waterfront – the fill meant that Front Street became distant from the water and no longer ran along the edge of the bay. During the first half of the twentieth century the precinct had been used for transportation and heavy manufacturing. Since the early 1950s it had been seen as expendable land, good only for expressways and open storage, even though its westerly edge touched Yonge Street only a handful of blocks south of King Street.

Stretching from Yonge to Parliament streets, from Front Street south to the railway tracks, the St Lawrence site proposed for redevelopment by the city was a mammoth forty-five acres. Development of this scale happened on almost a daily basis in the suburbs, but for Toronto large-scale development was thought to be of much smaller acreage, such as the twenty-six acres of Regent Park North, or the even smaller private development in St Jamestown. In both those cases, plans proposed to obliterate an existing community and replace it with something new. What was different about St Lawrence was that its planning was approached with the underlying assumption that it would become much like a traditional Toronto neighbourhood.

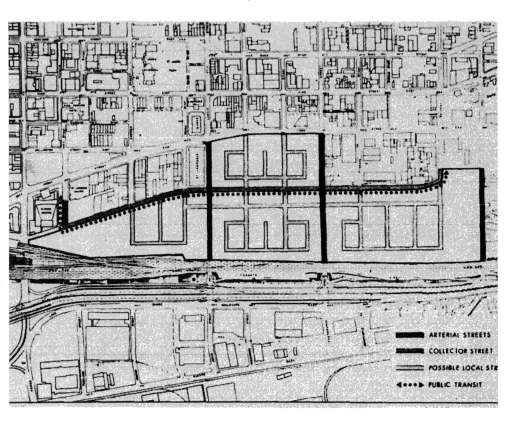

ARTERIAL STREETS
COLLECTOR STREET
POSSIBLE LOCAL STR
PUBLIC TRANSIT

St Lawrence community, street plan. This sketch shows the relationship of the St Lawrence site of Toronto's downtown. The westerly extremity of the site touches Yonge Street and is half a dozen blocks southeast of Bay and King streets, the heart of the city's financial district. The proposed street system picks up on the existing street pattern to the north – southern access is blocked by the main railway embankment leading into downtown. City of
Toronto Housing department

St Lawrence community under construction, 1978. In the foreground are townhouses; midground, a medium-rise apartment building; background, the banking towers of downtown. City of Toronto Housing Department

While the City of Toronto purchased the whole site for re-development purposes, perhaps the key to the plan ultimately arrived at was the decision-making process. Council established a committee that eschewed professional planning advice and prized ordinary citizen input. The committee consisted of representatives from neighbourhood groups, public housing projects, nonprofit cooperative housing, and the private development industry, as well as members of council from the wards affected. Planning staff and consultants reported to the committee, which carried the bulk of discussion around urban design principles and guidelines and reported regularly to council on its decisions. The approach taken by the committee was at considerable variance from modernist planning theory, since in this case the planner was fettered by a committee and was unable to exercise a free hand.

The first decision about form was that the development would respect Toronto's existing grid pattern rather than obliterate it in the manner of St Jamestown or Regent Park. Existing streets would be extended into St Lawrence and new streets would be created within that pattern, ensuring that the development would be integrated with, rather than isolated from, surrounding areas.

Second, buildings would face directly onto streets. No buildings would be hidden away on private thoroughfares, and, like every other city neighbourhood, front doors would have direct access to a public street by a walkway traversing a front yard.

Third, buildings would be designed on a human scale and at high densities. Much housing would be provided in a three-storey row house form traditional to Toronto, with front and back yards. Apartment buildings would be kept to about eight stories, except in unusual transitional locations such as at the corner of Yonge and Esplanade streets. Whereas suburban densities were usually less than ten units an acre, densities in St Lawrence were in the order of one hundred units per acre, considerably greater than even Regent Park North, at thirty units per acre.

Fourth, the development would contain a mix of uses, just like other city neighbourhoods. Schools, grocery stores, hair-

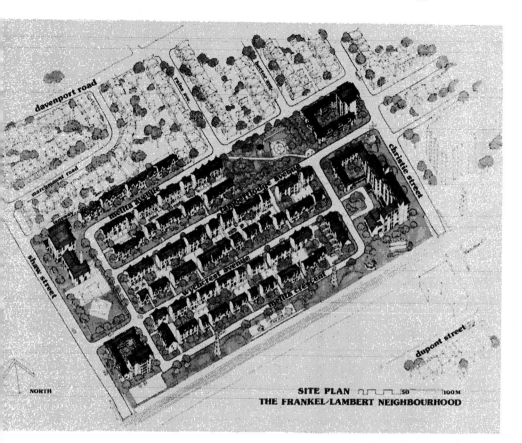

Frankel Lambert site plan. What is most clear is the ordinariness of the street system and the buildings that will line it: townhouses and small apartment structures, as well as a school (on Shaw Street) and an old-age home on Christie. City of Toronto Housing Department

dressers, cleaners, a dentist's office, a squash club, restaurants, and the like would be found at grade on main streets in St Lawrence and on appropriate corners. A linear park, which at some points also served as school playground, ran through the centre of the site, echoing the esplanade the city had hoped to establish in 1855 before railways overwhelmed that intention.

To ensure that the development fit into the existing city, urban design guidelines called for traditional forms and the use of red brick as an exterior cladding. Development parcels were devised to ensure that there would be a number of different developers who could retain architects, adding their own interpretations to this general framework. The result is that buildings provide a continuity, or variations on a theme, rather than the repetitious monotony of Regent Park North. As well, a variety of tenures and housing managers were provided, including private rental, nonprofit rental, nonprofit cooperative, fee simple ownership, and condominium ownership.

By 1976 construction was underway on the first of the 3500 units planned for the site, and within ten years 2500 units had been built east of Jarvis Street. Residents proclaimed it a great success, and private developers had no trouble selling or renting units alongside the coops and nonprofits. Worries were even expressed about property speculation at the edges of St Lawrence as developers looked to take advantage of more housing opportunities. St Lawrence quickly became known as the new community downtown that felt like it has always been there – which of course was exactly what the planning committee had intended.

St Lawrence stood as the successful example of an alternative to the modernist view. It refused to answer Stein's call for a new start, but instead took its lead from the older city to find a new idiom.

The establishment of the city's housing company, CityHome, permitted city council to continue this influence in many neighbourhoods. The style pursued was that developed in St Lawrence: respect for existing urban form, and attempts to strengthen this form by building structures that fit in rather than standing out. Another large redevelopment was under-

Wales Avenue City Home project. This is typical of housing built by the city
in the late 1970s and early 1980s: the housing units have a direct relationship to the street from walkways across a small front yard; the building is low
scale, with traditional design elements such as peaked and sloping roofs.
City of Toronto Housing Department

taken on the same planning principles – Frankel/Lambert, in the west end, again on a derelict industrial site. The scheme, reads a CityHome publication, 'is an extension of the existing neighbourhood: low rise apartments, row houses, private homes and a school and a park designed to appeal to the middle class neighbourhood of which it forms a part' (CityHome 9). Several dozen smaller projects built by CityHome in the next decade were modest in scale and concept, and also used traditional forms and materials.

As the CityHome publicity brochure states, 'The designs are planned to blend as much as possible into the existing neighbourhood from the viewpoints of architecture and social composition.' The new and different in planning had been supplanted by the tried and true.

A complete review of planning controls in most neighbourhoods was undertaken by city staff, beginning first with those neighbourhoods most under threat. The overriding theme in the new plans was that existing neighbourhoods should be strengthened. Official plan designations and zoning controls were amended to encourage change that fit in a neighbourhood, rather than change that destroyed and replaced. The emphasis was on infilling and smaller-scale projects, although the impetus for large-scale apartment structures as in St Jamestown was brought to a halt more by rent controls introduced by the provincial government in 1975 than by changes to planning instruments. These smaller neighbourhood plans echoed, at an appropriate scale, the grander vision of the Central Area Plan.

There was no mistaking the intention or the result of the reform wave that gained a foothold in the city in the early 1970s: the day of destroying the existing city to replace it with a New Jerusalem was over in Toronto. Alternatives were at hand, and they were much more attractive and comforting that the ideas of Howard, Wright, and Le Corbusier.

7

The Suburbs
Ascendant

Regardless of events in the city, modern planning was ascendant on the fringes of Toronto. Farmers' fields exploded with residential developments cloned from Don Mills, and a new generation of corporate suburbs emerged with sites larger and schemes more ambitious than Don Mills.

The provincial government responded by trying to control the extent of new development with the Toronto-Centred Region (TCR) Plan, which, however well conceived, failed for lack of political support. A second level of response emerged, including programs devised to protect farmland, to reduce the price of new homes, and to modify servicing standards to blunt the negative effects of low-density housing. None was effective.

Within Metro Toronto, as expressways were put on hold and transit subsidies rose inexorably, politicians looked for ways to contain sprawl. They opted to encourage subcentres in the newly developed suburbs, and those policies met with some success. But beyond Metro's boundaries, where provincial programs were seen to support and encourage low-density development, there was no counterweight of public opinion against modern planning ideas and they could be implemented without restraint.

The opportunity for expansive suburban development had first been noted by none other than E.P. Taylor. In 1955, barely three years into the eight-year construction schedule needed to complete Don Mills, Taylor purchased 8700 acres of farmland to the west of Toronto. This tract was destined to become the largest new development seen in southern Ontario, Erin Mills.

Fifteen years lapsed between purchase and development, fifteen years of significant development activity in the Toronto area. The Corporation of Metropolitan Toronto, an innovative federation of thirteen municipalities, was created by the provincial government in 1953 as an alternative to one large amalgamated urban area. Metro (as it quickly became known) had responsibility for regional functions such as planning, policing, sewage and water treatment, and joint capital borrowing; the local municipalities continued to provide functions such as garbage pickup and parks, as well as development approval.

Metro's greatest strength was its ability to borrow for the expansion of suburban services against the wealth of Toronto's downtown, thus permitting the rapid expansion of the large boroughs around Toronto – Scarborough, North York, and Etobicoke. Combined with the servicing arrangements pioneered in Don Mills – the developer assumed responsibly for all local improvements such as roads and pipes as well as land dedications for roads, parks, and school sites – this borrowing capacity permitted substantial urban growth to keep up with new household formation.

The growth was phenomenal. By 1971 North York's population exceeded half a million – from a mere 85,000 in 1951. Scarborough and Etobicoke grew almost as quickly, from a combined population of 110,000 in 1951 to 535,000 in 1971 (Spelt 1973, 85). In North York, commercial and residential real estate assessment quadrupled between 1954 and 1966 to more than $1 billion, which was only slightly less than half Toronto's total assessment in 1966. During the same period, development in Scarborough and Etobicoke tripled the taxable assessment of both municipalities (Spelt 1973, 88).

Without exception, development stuck within the precepts of modern planning. Residential form followed Don Mills: the curvy streets now seen on maps of Toronto mark the break in the mid 1950s as the influence of Don Mills becomes apparent, contrasting with the straight residential streets that had predominated until that time. Much land was set aside for nonresidential uses, whether in Scarborough's Golden Mile – a 1950s strip of commercial and industrial enterprises on Eglinton Avenue – or in the industrial expanses of Etobicoke along the Queen Elizabeth highway, which linked directly into the Gardiner Expressway early in the 1960s.

Development sites within Metro were generally at a smaller scale than Don Mills, with developers owning sites of several hundred rather than several thousand acres. But the Don Mills schematic was used, most frequently in Scarborough, where John Bousfield served as the commissioner of planning during the 1950s. Development parcels were planned in larger sections so that residential road patterns could be continuous among different developers, and so the ring road around a shopping plaza could encircle the intersection of two arterials where quadrants might be owned by four different development companies. From a distance of several decades, it now seems as though development schemes in Scarborough were large scale, covering thousands of acres, but that effect is a result of comprehensive planning concepts imposed by the municipality on a number of development sites of several hundred acres apiece.

One rare example of a larger-scale development occurred on 1700 acres assembled in 1953 by the provincial and federal governments for the community of Malvern, in the northeast area of Scarborough. The site was not planned until development had spread to its edges in the late 1960s, and construction was not completed until the end of the decade. Planning was undertaken by Project Planning Associates, Macklin Hancock's company. 'One of the principal objects of the Malvern plan is to create a unified, imaginative, balanced and attractive urban environment,' reads the planning document (Community Development Consultants [1971], 15), but even though it was a publicly sponsored scheme, presumably free of the financial rigours constraining private firms, it showed little innovation save for the scattered sprinkling of low-income public housing units.

The immense amount of activity within Metro Toronto led some developers to look for opportunities outside Metro's boundaries. The area to the west of Toronto was favoured, perhaps because of proximity to the city's airport in Malton as air travel and traffic increased.

In 1958, 5200 acres of land to the north and west of Toronto was acquired for a community of 50,000 residents to be called Bramalea. The proposal was planned by John W. Galbraith and Company, an American firm billed as 'one of North America's largest urban developers,' and it was touted as 'Canada's first satellite city' (Bramalea Consolidated Development 1958; Bureau of Municipal Research, Civic Affairs, no. 2, 1972: 17). A decade later, after 12,000 residents and forty-four factories were in place, the company revised its description to 'Canada's first suburban city' and projected an ultimate population in the range of 100,000.

Apart from size, there was little innovative about Bramalea. It is a Levittown based on a Don Mills model, with the same looped roads, separation of uses, low densities, and profusion of open space. It was sold with crass hype, the company promising 'unparalleled livability.' No master plan was demanded by the municipality, nor was one ever put on paper. The company preferred, as it noted on several occasions, to permit 'utmost flexibility,' as in doubling population projections.

When it was planned a decade later, Erin Mills showed more imagination and attention. The first report on water and sewer needs was in 1957, only two years after the assembly began, and by 1961 the Mississauga Council enacted Official Plan Amendment 114, approving urban development for the site. Five years later the Metro Toronto Planning Board, which then possessed advisory planning powers in neighbouring townships outside its formal jurisdiction of Metro Toronto, also agreed, and Don Mills Development Corporation, owner of the site, began its serious planning exercise.

Planning for Erin Mills was done by an illustrious team. Chief planner was Eli Comay, formerly Metro's planning commissioner and creator of planning guidelines for the Jane/Finch corridor in North York. Working with him were James Murray, architect in Don Mills and a leader in the Canadian Housing Design Council; John Bousfield, formerly head of the Planning Department in Scarborough and at this time one of the leading planning consultants in Ontario; and John Daniels, later architect and partner in the Cadillac Fairview Development Corporation, one of Canada's largest development companies.

Promotional material from the company called Erin Mills 'one of the most imaginative planned communities on the continent,' accommodating 170,000 people in the ten square miles of the assembly. Rather than make it a self-contained community – the failed goal of Don Mills – it would be an extension of the existing urban area, as the planners noted in the company's planning book:

Erin Mills will not be a 'new town' or 'satellite town' in the classic British or Swedish sense, primarily because it will be an integral part of the metropolitan area rather than separated from it by a wide belt of open countryside. It will represent a finger of urbanization extending out from the main body of urban development, bordered by major elements of open land, and will possess many of the distinctive features of the best new towns. (Don Mills Development Corporation 1969)

Excluding commercial, industrial, and institutional areas, residential densities were planned at twenty-seven persons per acre – somewhat less than Don Mills. Just as Hancock had proposed a mix of incomes and housing forms for Don Mills to meet planning rather than market objectives, the planners here made the case for smaller rather than larger homes. 'The modest sized single family house on a smaller lot is worthy of reconsideration,' the planning booklet noted. 'When houses are arranged in a group or cluster form, a property 40 x 100 feet is quite adequate for even a three bedroom 1200 square foot single storey residence.' This is one of the rare instances where the planners argued against even lower densities than might otherwise be built.

Of the 50,000 units to be built, 40 per cent would be low-density single family houses, 37 per cent apartments, and the remainder in multiple-unit structures such as semi-detached homes, row housing, and duplexes. This housing mix was considerably more intense and varied than usual for the 1960s – slightly more than thirteen units per net acre when most suburban housing developments of single family homes on large lots were at densities of seven or eight units per acre. In many respects the Erin Mills plan is a return to the idealism of Don Mills, where the mix is comparable: 56 per cent of Don Mills's units are in three-storey apartment buildings, and perhaps 20 per cent in row and semi-detached housing. The difference is one of form – the apartments contemplated in Erin Mills would be fifteen or more stories high.

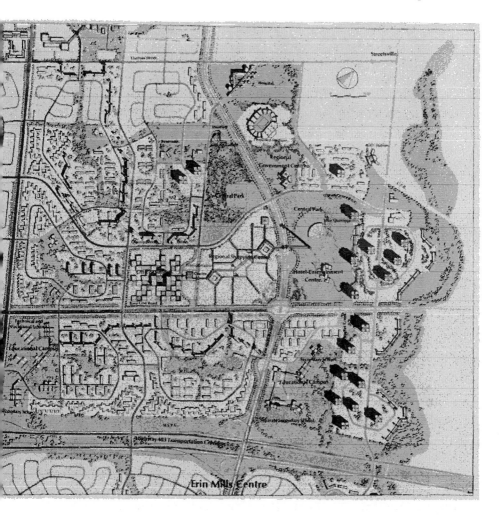

Erin Mills central area plan. This plan includes offices, government centres, educational campus, as well as large apartment towers and smaller residential blocks. The roads are relatively few, the road system is discontinuous, and structures bear virtually no relationship to them. Metropolitan Toronto Reference Library

TABLE 1

General Land Uses in Erin Mills and Don Mills

Use	Erin Mills		Don Mills	
	Acres	Per cent	Acres	Per cent
Housing	3,780	43	800	38
Open space	960	11	400	19
Commercial	415	5	75	3
Industrial	960	11	320	16
Institutional	840	9	145	7
Roads	1,775	21	320	16
Total acres	8,730		2,060	

One important difference with Don Mills is open space: formally there would be 50 per cent less in Erin Mills, although it would be augmented by the large private open spaces surrounding the planned apartment towers. A second difference is the amount of land devoted to industrial parks, which had proved a valuable use, even if, as had been learned in Don Mills, local residents did not work there. The difference in land for road designation may be accounted for by land already secured by the provincial government for several expressways crossing the site.

The similarities with Don Mills far outweigh the differences. What differs in this 'second generation' of suburban development is the scale: like Bramalea, Erin Mills is far bigger and far more ambitious than Don Mills. But like Don Mills, the plan was changed in its execution, which took two decades. Far fewer apartment and smaller house-form units were constructed than planned, since the market for single family houses was so strong. Thus the expressed desire for more modest units and a mixed social structure was not fully realized.

Construction of Erin Mills began in 1971 and Ontario premier William Davis attended the opening of the first buildings, providing his political blessing:

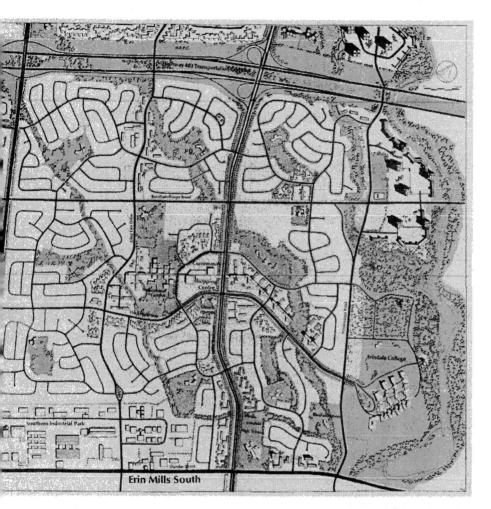

Erin Mills neighbourhood plan. Many streets loop back on themselves, becoming private enclaves rather than public thoroughfares that might actually lead somewhere. Metropolitan Toronto Reference Library.

I am particularly excited about this kind of development. It is
creative, imaginative, and takes into account the many social
changes taking place today ... It is the kind of development of which
Mississauga can be proud, of which the Province of Ontario can be
proud, but more importantly, the people living in it will find it a
truly human experience. (*Erin Mills Newsletter*, spring 1981)

Davis was stretching a point in claiming provincial pride for
this kind of development. What had been previously expressed
by the province, loudly and clearly, was concern. For almost a
decade the province feared it might not be able to service this
kind of development, and worried about how alternatives might
be put in place.

In 1962 the provincial government began the Metro Toronto
and Region Transportation Study. MTARTS, as it began to be
known, looked at transportation policy in the light of expected
population growth in the Toronto area. In 1962, 2.4 million
residents lived in the census metropolitan area: population
projections increased that number to between 5 million and 6.2
million by the year 2000 (Fraser et al. 1974). MTARTS began
simply looking at transportation, but added to it was a land-use
component, provided by Professor Len Gertler.

Working with staff at the Municipal Affairs ministry, Gertler
completed a report entitled 'Choices for a Growing Region,'
which considered two main growth strategies as alternatives to
the status quo, each with different variants. One strategy called
for growth entirely along the lake, from Bowmanville on the
east to Hamilton on the west. The second strategy called for
growth along the lake, with a second tier of municipalities,
divided from the first tier by a parkway belt, slightly to the
north.

MTARTS was never intended to be more than a study, providing basic information on which decisions might be made, and
these reports did not lead to action. Then, in 1966, a new turn
was taken by Premier John Robarts, with the establishment of
Design for Development. This was a broad, multifaceted planning exercise, dealing with very basic planning choices. As one
participant noted:

Its primary aim [was] to stimulate economic growth in the less favoured regions [of Ontario]. The 'design' was essentially an organizational one. No new programs were announced. Indeed, the crucial feature of the 'design' was that the resources devoted to existing programs, ranging from water to education, were of such magnitude as to be effective as an instrument of regional development policy given the necessary coordination. (Cullingworth 1984, 143)

A staff team was established within the Ministry of Municipal Affairs to prepare plans for ten economic regions in the province. The process was driven by Ian Macdonald, appointed in 1965 as chief economist for the province; planner Nigel Richardson, working with others such as Hans Blumenfeld; and Darcy McKeough, appointed minister of municipal affairs in 1967. For our purposes, the key document developed under this process was the Toronto-Centred Region Plan, released in 1970.

Exactly what this planning process was to focus on was not entirely clear: the mandate was extremely broad. Robarts gave some emphasis to structural questions, indicating that Design for Development was 'planning a closer relationship of regional economic development and the structure of local government' (Richardson 1984, 129). Macdonald, however, said:

We are concerned in the Toronto-Centred Region Plan not only with the need for foresight, but also with the capacity to sort out a complex of forces as complicated as putting a man on the moon. In its simplest terms we are seeking to decide the nature, character and quality of life to which we might aspire in the province, and more importantly, which we can pass on to our children and grandchildren. (Richardson 1984, 94)

McKeough, who provided the leadership within the government, was more precise in focusing on physical planning questions:

The problems associated with rapid urbanization are particularly apparent in the Toronto-Centred Region. Land prices are escalating so rapidly that an increasing number of people are facing great difficulty in financing a home of their own; or alternatively, are having to live long distances away from their place of work, and commute for several hours a day. Congestion, pollution and noise are increasing at an alarming rate, accompanied by a deterioration in certain neighbourhoods and a loss of the highly valued sense of community identity. (McKeough 1971, 1)

In fact, the work of the group produced a 'detailed program of analysis which revealed how each part of the province compared with the provincial average in terms of sixty-three separate statistical indicators' (Richardson 1981, 566). In the first five years, one development policy was produced – for northwestern Ontario – as well as the Toronto-Centred Region Plan. The plan was seen as a provincial initiative, not as a joint exercise between provincial and local planning staff, and that meant that local politicians – always wary of how provincial schemes might affect them – greeted it with suspicion.

The TCR Plan created three zones: Zone 1, Urban Complex, an urbanized area along the lakeshore, running from east of Oshawa west to Hamilton; Zone 2, Rural and Recreational, a recreational, agricultural, and open-space zone surrounding the urbanized area; and Zone 3, Selective Growth, an outer zone covering land within a ninety-minute drive of Toronto. As a later planning document noted, there were four key concepts that affected Zone 1, the urbanized area:

1. Two tiers of urban communities parallel to the lakeshore, separated by a parkway belt, and varying in scale and function.
2. A strong east-west linear configuration, anchored at either end by Oshawa and Hamilton as second order centres, with Toronto as the first-order or primate centre.
3. Stimulation of eastward growth, matched by restraint of development northward in the Yonge Street corridor.
4. A broad tract in the north (Zone 2) to remain predominantly rural. (Central Ontario Lakeshore Urban Complex [COLUC] Report, 3)

A significant problem the plan tried to address was the difficulty of servicing the area to the north of Toronto, where there was considerable development pressure. Water and sewage services were much easier to provide to municipalities with direct access to Lake Ontario than to those blocked from the lake by Metro Toronto – hence the dampening of development expectations in Zone 2 and the encouragement of development to the east of the city.

In a statement made in 1971, a year after the plan had been released publicly, McKeough said:

For the foreseeable future, therefore, the major urbanized area of the Toronto-Centred Region will be limited to the two-tiered system of centres as outlined for Zone 1 in the initial report – the lakeshore tier of urban communities and the northern tier adjacent to the Parkway Belt system. Within the single labour and housing market of this urbanized area, it is the Government's intention to stimulate growth in the eastern corridor to reduce to some degree the pressure in Metropolitan Toronto and to a lesser extent the western corridor, both of which are showing the effects of congestion and excessive land prices.

Not all of the area in Zone 1 is suited to immediate large scale growth. The provision of trunk services, whether sewers, water, transit or communications is expensive and must be rationalized. Centres in Zone 1 will not be allowed to expand to their ultimate capacity immediately. In general we will assist and encourage growth in a compact form, properly staged by the economies of servicing. (McKeough 1971, 6)

The plan attempted to encourage a compact form to ensure efficiency in public spending on matters such as servicing and transit. In addition, one of its explicit goals was 'to facilitate and maintain a pattern of identifiable communities.' New suburban development did not create self-contained, self-sufficient communities.

But the plan was not, in the end, decisive. The many developers who had already assembled land in the expectation of obtaining development rights wished to receive approvals rather than rebuffs. Local politicians who saw the future of their own communities, as well as their own personal political future, in growing rather than in being constrained castigated the plan as yet another unwelcome attempt by the provincial government to intervene in local affairs. Hampering the situation was the fact that implementation proposals were not part of the plan, making it very difficult for the government to move forward with dispatch. Richardson thought the plan's weakness was mostly structural:

The fundamental weakness of provincial planning lay in its failure either to become an integral part of the governmental system, or to win wholehearted support at the political level, within the provincial bureaucracy, or from any broader political or popular constituency. (Richardson 1981, 563)

The TCR plan was never abandoned, but it languished. In 1973 the province announced it was proceeding with the proposed parkway belt that would provide some separation between communities in Zone 1, helping to create the structure for the five-pole concept. At the same time, the province announced funding for the South Central (York-Durham) Servicing Scheme, a pipe snaking from the east of Metro at the lakeshore to beyond Metro's northern boundary, then heading west and north up Yonge Street. At the lake side, the piped corridor could treat sewage and provide drinking water. This would give needed water and sewage capacity to permit land immediately to the north of Metro to be developed, in direct contravention of the TCR plan (see COLUC, 4). The Parkway Belt was squeezed by urban development on both sides, and landowners battled to keep their parcels outside the designated zone, often successfully. Within a decade the Parkway Belt had been battered into little more than a thin grey servicing corridor. Any restraint to development north of Metro in the Yonge Street corridor was lifted. Markham, for which TCR predicted a population of about 20,000 by 1990, had 100,000 residents by 1985 (McKeough 1971, 12).

A review of the plan was undertaken in 1974 by the Central

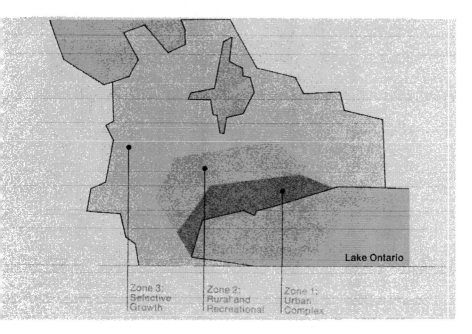

Zone 3: Selective Growth | Zone 2: Rural and Recreational | Zone 1: Urban Complex

Lake Ontario

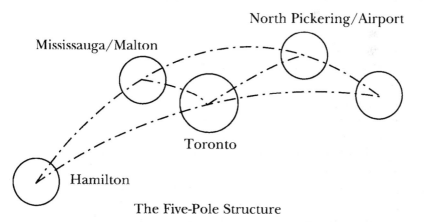

North Pickering/Airport

Mississauga/Malton

Toronto

Hamilton

The Five-Pole Structure

The Toronto-Centred Region concept was utter simplicity: the city's attempt to spread would be limited by a broad greenbelt, beyond which selective growth would be permitted. Richardson 1984. The five-pole structure was more complicated, but it again denied city spread, hoping to keep the five poles as distinct and separate places. Central Ontario Lakeshore Urban Complex 1974

Ontario Lakeshore Urban Complex (COLUC) task force. It all but admitted the TCR plan had been abandoned. The large-scale attempt to contain the new suburban form had failed.

Two indirect attacks on suburban form were made at the provincial level, but, as with the TCR plan, both had little effect. One responded to the concern that too much farmland was being turned into suburban subdivisions – estimates as high as fourteen acres moving from farm uses to suburban sprawl every hour were voiced. One goal of the TCR plan had been to minimize the urban use of productive agricultural land. In 1978 the Ontario government set out Food Land Guidelines intended to serve as one measure of whether quality agricultural land should be developed. The guidelines required municipalities to inventory farmland and give high priority to the protection of productive land, 'to ensure the best lands are kept for agricultural use' (Ministry of Agriculture and Food 1978, Section 3.2). But the Food Land Guidelines never became more than informal government policy, and while they provided a hoop through which the developer had to jump when making his case, they rarely figured in the retention of land in the face of development pressure.

The other attempt to rework suburbia related to the high price of housing. As noted earlier, house prices rose considerably in the 1960s, and even more so in the 1970s.

TABLE 2
House Prices in the Metro Toronto Area

Year	Suburban House Price	Metro Average House Price	Metro Average Family Income
1953	$11,600	$14,000	$5,400
1963	19,000	16,000	6,542
1971	35,000	30,426	11,841
1981	120,000	90,203	31,238

Source: Sewell 1992

The price of a new suburban home had risen from about twice average family income in 1953 to three times by 1971, and four times by 1981. The average for Metro had remained fairly constant at three times family income. How could the rising price of suburban housing be moderated?

There is a vast literature on suburban land assemblies of the 1960s and 1970s, attempting to settle the question of whether an oligarchy existed that drove up land prices (see particularly Spurr 1976; Markusen and Scheffman 1977; and Lorimer 1978.) Whether a few companies had enough control of the market to raise prices was not something anyone seemed capable of proving beyond another's doubt – although a strong case was made that a few companies owned a great deal of land ready to be developed – and thus, while there was talk about a speculation tax, there was no action.

Since a large portion of the cost of a new home was attributed to land – the price of the lot equalled about 40 per cent of the sale price of a new suburban house (Lorimer 1978) – one theory was that a better, more intense use of land could result in low house prices. In 1976 the Ministry of Housing produced a study, *Urban Development Standards*, which showed that many steps could be taken to improve the use of land. This study recommended that net residential densities be increased from 6.5 units per acre – the conventional density of new suburbs in Ontario – to 12.5 (47), resulting in a significant cost saving for land. As well, municipal standards for road widths and the like could be modified downwards, producing an environment that was certainly no worse. The study argued that, 'compared to conventional practices, our proposed standards and cost comparisons include increased landscaping and privacy screening, more park space landscaped for children's play and improved control over design and siting of individual units' (ii).

Few municipalities implemented the new standards, although in some instances individual developers used elements of them in developments. The values of the new suburbs were not to be so easily upset, nor were the practices of developers who had learned to work profitably within the new planning systems. That land was being squandered, that house and lot designs could be improved, that house prices could be reduced – these seemed not to be the concerns of those in positions to make decisions.

More success at reshaping suburban form was found at the local level. The main push came, not unexpectedly, from the City of Toronto. Expressway pressures had already been re-buffed with the defeat of the Spadina Expressway and the shelving of the Scarborough Expressway a few years later, but city politicians found (almost to their surprise) that their pre-ferred transportation option, public transit, was not readily supported by their counterparts in the suburbs. The recognition that there were two different kinds of cities in the one urban area dawned only slowly.

The city built before the Second World War was just about perfect for public transit. The grid road system with its small blocks gave excellent opportunities for straight routes where the turning of the transit vehicles was kept to a minimum. Densities of fifteen to twenty units per acre meant that enough people lived along each route to provide a ready customer base to pay for the service. Mixed land uses – retail strips for shopping, a dispersed commercial and industrial base – meant that destinations were not always distant, and a considerable number of rides were short.

The modern suburb, by contrast, was not so amenable to transit. Low densities produced few potential riders for each mile travelled, and journeys were often long enough to be uncomfortable. The discontinuous road system made it difficult to plan reasonable transit routes close to where people lived. As a result, the rational suburban resident used a private car for transportation needs.

The different approaches to transportation came out clearly in questions of funding. Suburban politicians wanted public money put into roads, whereas city politicians preferred transit. Since the provincial government had stopped innercity ex-pressway funding with the announcement to abandon the Spadina Expressway, the dispute centred on how transit should be funded: from the fare box (through increased fares) or through property taxes.

For several decades the Toronto Transit Commission dealt

with the higher costs associated with transit service to the newer suburbs by charging a double fare, using a two-zone system with the dividing line virtually coincident with development patterns until 1945. The system worked well: while providing good service to the city and the suburbs alike, the TCR operated in the black, without public operating subsidies from 1921 to 1970. The double fare paid the extra costs involved in providing service to the suburbs.

That changed in 1972. One provincial concession to the suburbs when the decision to stop the Spadina Expressway was made was to end the double fare system and institute a single fare system throughout Metro, and to improve transit service to suburban areas. The cost of these changes has been striking. The TTC's deficit shot from $2.9 million in 1971 to $49.0 million in 1976; it breached the $100 million mark in the early 1980s and exceeded $200 million in 1991. After fifty years operating on a break-even basis, public transit in Toronto became a major drain on the tax dollar.

In 1971, with the Spadina Expressway decision clearly on its mind, Metro Council undertook a study, funded in conjunction with the TTC and the Ministry of Transportation and Communication, to review 'the relationship between the nature and magnitude of development and the rate at which transportation facilities can be provided' (Soberman 1975, 3). The study also reviewed the financing of transportation and how better transit could be provided. The Metro Toronto Transportation Plan Review was directed by Professor Richard Soberman. Soberman noted, 'There are ... likely to be some serious problems in [Metro] meeting the annual commitments for increasing [transit] deficits if substantial fare increases are not to be introduced' (15).

MTTPR looked at transportation choices – expressways, intermediate capacity transit, commuter rail – and related them to alternative land-use strategies. In the Summary Report issued in 1975, Soberman argued there were really only two choices: continued centralization, with an intense downtown surrounded by residential suburbs, or decentralization. He thought four development possibilities existed for the decentralization option: bi-nodal, with a second commercial centre to be developed to the north of downtown, in Downsview; regional subcentres, in North York, Scarborough, and northern Mississauga (probably Brampton and its suburb Bramalea); corridor development, along several main arteries; and dispersed development, where commercial development happened in a sprawling fashion. A total of twenty-three different combinations of transportation and land-use alternatives were reviewed for considerations such as cost, social and economic implications, environmental impact, and development feasibility.

The report recommended a subcentre approach, concluding it 'provides major job opportunities at more locations throughout the Metropolitan area than any other alternative, and therefore maximizes the choice of job opportunities available to residents. It also maximizes the use of public transit in suburban areas and provides for the best utilization of major transit facilities in both directions' (Soberman 1975, 85).

Overshadowing this change of direction were the recommendations about expressways: the Spadina Expressway should not be revived; the Scarborough Expressway should be abandoned; and the Highway 400 extension, serving the northwest part of the city, should probably not be proceeded with. Suburban politicians, who now dominated Metro Council, were not pleased, and the report was not acted on.

The struggle for suburban form was taken up by Toronto City Council. The thinking that was emerging around the Central Area Plan in 1974 and 1975 was that the downtown should be a mixed area of housing and offices. Planners worried that unless the demand for new office space downtown was dampened, the opportunity to establish viable housing would be limited, since housing could never attract the land price available to office uses.

Deconcentration – the word coined to signify a movement away from downtown concentration – was the agreed-upon tool: planners recommended that policies be set in place to encourage office uses that did not really require a central location to go elsewhere. Functions fitting this category would be regional offices, computer processing, and other parts of companies that didn't require face-to-face contact. Planners hoped to encourage deconcentration by limiting the amount of new office space permitted in the downtown and by establishing other locations with comparable attractions.

Hence the idea of creating 'downtowns in the suburbs,' or subcentres, to use Soberman's terminology. Instead of just shopping malls, the subcentre should be a mixed-use area where people would work, live, shop, and be entertained. For Toronto planners, such areas could be the recipients of the office space deflected from the downtown. An added advantage would be a reduced need by suburbanites to commute, and a concomitant reduced demand for new expressways.

These ideas were embodied in Toronto's Central Area Plan. Since that plan needed the approval of Metro Council, which had regional planning responsibilities – and the Central Area Plan certainly had regional planning significance – Mayor David Crombie made a point of talking to his counterparts in Scarborough and North York to ensure they did not object. After much discussion and hand-holding, the mayors of those municipalities agreed to support the plan, although they seemed not to recognize that changing the idea of modernist planning forms might provoke new and positive development opportunities.

By the end of the decade, the subcentre idea had become common wisdom, and it became official policy in Metroplan, the general plan adopted by Metro Council in 1980. It was dubbed the Centres policy, and stated that such areas should be multi-functional (including office, commercial, and residential uses), compact, pedestrian oriented, and intensely developed (Metropolitan Toronto Planning Department 1980, Sec. 4c). The modern idea of separated, segregated uses was put to one side. One centre would be located in North York along Yonge Street, between Sheppard and Finch avenues; the other in the Scarborough Town Centre (later renamed City Centre). Politicians in North York and Scarborough quickly recognized that with virtually all residential land in the municipality developed, the only way to keep growing would be by redevelopment.

Redevelopment of these areas followed their designation as centres. The area chosen for North York's downtown was a strip shopping district built in the early 1950s, surrounded by streets set in a grid pattern (it was built a few years before Don Mills) and lined with single-family ranch-style houses. Within a decade, more than a dozen large residential and/or commercial towers were built in the North York subcentre, with another dozen in the proposal or planning stage. North York mayor Mel Lastman revelled in the negotiations and deal-making involved, as well as in fending off local citizen opposition to the changes in building form (the new towers loomed over surrounding neighbourhoods) and increased automobile traffic. While complaints exist about the nature of the change – little thought has been given to creating a pleasant pedestrian environment – the opportunities for a successful suburban downtown seem apparent.

The change proposed for the Scarborough City Centre has proven more difficult. The urban fabric requiring reshaping was a carefully planned 1960s shopping centre, surrounded by belts of land allocated for office uses and green space, all in classical modernist style. Adding new uses – a hotel, some office buildings, then housing – did not create a compact, intense, pedestrian-oriented area but a collection of isolated structures with different uses. The privately owned concourse of the shopping centre continued to be the only area attractive to pedestrians, and during the late 1980s it proved the location of choice for teenage gangs to stage their encounters. In spite of good intentions, a 'downtown' has yet to be created in the Scarborough City Centre. It is the centre only in a geographical sense.

Metroplan, adopted in 1980, did more than simply define a new Centres policy. It also outlined opposition to continued growth of 'office parks,' those collections of nonresidential uses found bunched at the intersections of main roadways. Office parks were the nonresidential equivalent of the residential suburb: a segregated commercial area, at low density, reliant on the private automobile, with a discontinuous road system. Metro planners noted the extent to which they generated automo-

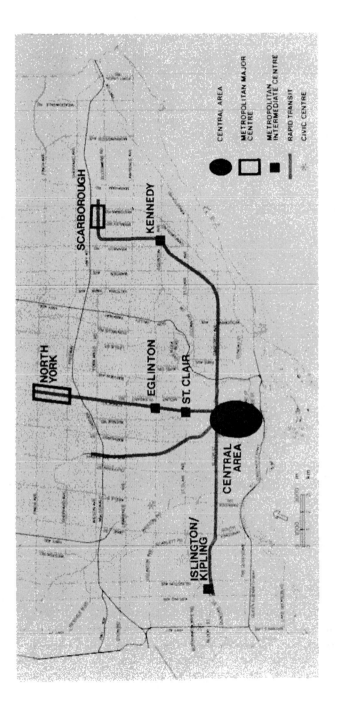

Metroplan Centres. The plan shows how the proposed centres within Metro will be linked to one another by rapid transit.
Metro Planning Department

bile traffic that was not easily displaced by transit, and thus created large roadway expenditures. Curtailing the growth of office parks would help to control transportation capital costs. Metroplan proposed that no further office parks be permitted.

One section of Metroplan took direct issue with low-density residential development. Section 7B7 of the new plan provided that the minimum density for any development site larger than five acres would be fifteen units per acre – a density more than twice traditional suburban densities. While this statement was agreed to when the plan was originally considered at council, it was deleted in 1981 when politicians found it stood in the way of fast approval of subdivision plans for smaller sites.

While these changes considerably modified the form of the city within Metro, they had no effect on the bulk of suburban development that was then occurring outside Metro's boundaries, in the regions of Peel, York, and Durham. Those regional governments had been created by the provincial government in the early 1970s as an afterthought of the Design for Development process, in the expectation they could provide direction to suburban growth. But these regions didn't much care about the debates within Metro on the most appropriate or best urban form – indeed, neither Peel nor York adopted an official plan, as required by law, relying instead on an individual review of development applications rather than an overall policy approach. It meant that those planning in the new style had a free and unrestrained hand.

The devices needed to modify form outside Metro could only be set in place by the province, but it had already given up such attempts, as the Toronto-Centred Region Plan faded into the past. In the jurisdictions beyond Metro, the planning ideas in gestation since the end of the nineteenth century reigned triumphant, beyond the reach of their critics.

8

Redesign

The culture of modern planning, like all other cultures, will ultimately fade and be replaced. Exactly when and how that happens, or how long it continues to be dominant, remains to be seen: predicting reasons for the decline of a cultural fashion is rarely successful since decline often occurs because of quite unanticipated events and influences.

In the Toronto suburbs of the early 1990s, modern planning is undergoing substantial strains and is subject to growing criticism. Arguments are made that the results of modern planning are not publicly cost-effective, the social products are undesirable, the environment is damaged, and the housing created is too expensive for the market. These claims will be briefly touched on in this chapter, not so much to argue their merit in final fashion as to provide a context in which to discuss the design solutions emerging as alternatives to the corporate suburb.

Several eminent social critics have argued that physical form does not influence social behaviour. 'We must root out of thinking the assumption that the physical form of our communities has social consequence,' wrote the American sociologist Nathan Glazer in 1965 (cited in Fowler 1992, 72). Herbert Gans, as Fowler also notes, takes the same view, concluding, 'the planner has only limited influence over social relationships' (Fowler 1992, 71).

Other critics, however, have spent considerable energy studying the effect of form on behaviour, particularly in publicly sponsored housing projects. Oscar Newman, in *Defensible Space* and other books, has shown that modifying the form of highrise apartment structures in New York can have measurable positive social results: crime is lower, and feelings of personal safety are increased. Alice Coleman makes very persuasive arguments in *Utopia on Trial* that the design of low-rise council housing projects in London creates undesirable social behaviour such as littering, graffiti, damage from vandalism, and the presence (or omnipresence) of human urine and faeces. Her prescriptions for change include removal of overhead walkways; making individual blocks of housing autonomous by getting rid of 'confused space' that no one really seems to control; reducing anonymity and escape routes; and improving entrances and streetscape (Coleman 1985, 137ff). Coleman refutes arguments that these problems are caused by high densities, a surfeit of low-income households, or too many mother-led families.

There are more than one hundred public housing projects in Metro Toronto, many of which have been cited frequently as socially undesirable places – whether in the Jane/Finch area or in the downtown urban renewal projects noted in chapter 4. The projects are the locale of considerable drug dealing; are considered by residents to be generally unsafe places to live; and often have the appearance of being unkept and badly maintained in the sense Coleman describes.

In 1987 the Metro Toronto Housing Authority (MTHA), the agency responsible for managing the projects, undertook three studies on redesign possibilities. None of the studies has yet received the provincial support needed for implementation, although all have been given considerable endorsement from project residents. The studies show how modernist forms can be reshaped in the expectation that problems of social behaviour can be minimized.

Edgeley Village, in the Jane/Finch area, was designed in the 1960s by Irving Grossman, who was also responsible for the renovation of Alpha Avenue (see chapter 6). It consists of townhouses on a private road system and one twelve-storey apartment tower. Edgeley Village is like other public housing projects in Ontario: the land it occupies is all privately controlled – owned by the Ontario Housing Corporation and managed by MTHA, both bodies controlled by the Ontario government. This makes police surveillance very difficult. Canada, like other countries deriving its justice system from Britain, restricts police presence and permits them to enter private property only if specifically invited or in hot pursuit. Thus, normal police patrol is not possible within Edgeley Village, and even if it was, it would be difficult because of the lack of a through road system.

Since streets and sidewalks are private, ordinary municipal services such as street lighting, street cleaning, garbage collection, and road and sidewalk maintenance are provided by the

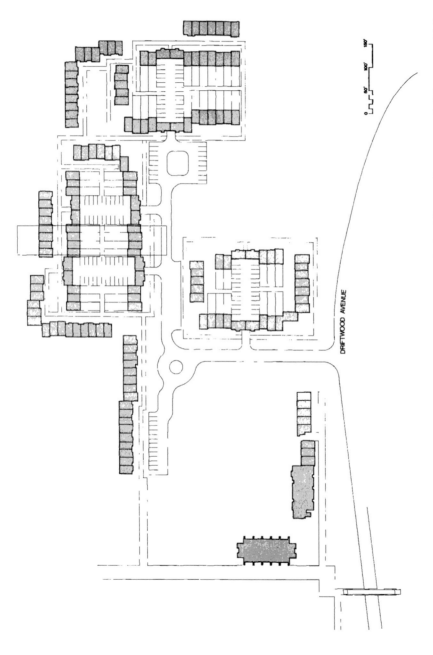

DRIFTWOOD AVENUE

Edgeley, 1991. The building footprints – all are two or three storeys, save for the building at the extreme left bottom, which is twelve storeys – show the divorce of residences from public streets: almost all homes are set on private walkways.

Alan Littlewood

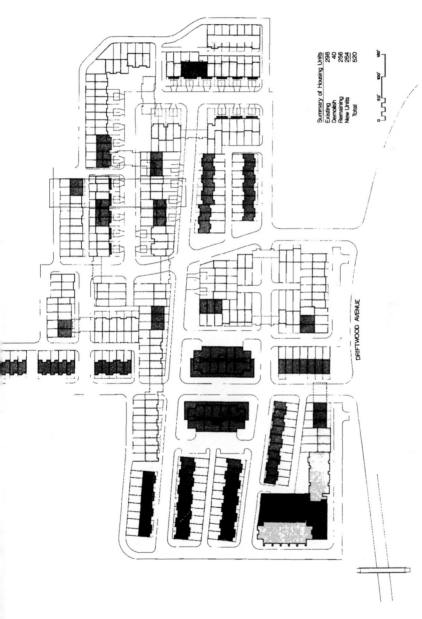

Edgeley scheme. Alan Littlewood, 1987. The dark markings show new structures; the white existing structures. Littlewood has extended the public street system so virtually every home fronts directly on a public street. With the exception of the two major dark buildings (which are six storeys), all other structures are two or three storeys. Alan Littlewood

DRIFTWOOD AVENUE

Summary of Housing Units	
Existing	298
Demolish	40
Remaining	256
New Units	264
Total	520

0   50'   100'   150'

landlord, not the municipality. Residents complain MTHA provides a standard of service for these common elements far below what neighbours have come to expect from the municipality. Without a street system, other urban services such as taxi pick-up and pizza delivery are virtually nonexistent because of the lack of street addresses. Management finds it difficult to control car parking, and up to a third of parking spaces in most projects are occupied by derelict vehicles.

Planner Alan Littlewood assumed these problems were mostly caused by the modernist notion of surrounding structures with a surfeit of green space and a denial of any public realm. The terms of reference under which he was asked to provide a redesign of Edgeley were:

- The introduction of public streets
- Construction on empty land
- Reduction of surface parking
- Entrance to dwellings directly off streets
- Creation of front and back yards
- Introduction of nonresidential units
- Increase in the number of units
- Clarification of public versus private areas
  (Sewell 1988, 121)

Littlewood's remedial plan is based around a public street system and a clear definition of public and private space. Parking would be regularized – either on the new public streets where normal policing could deal with it effectively, or in private yards where the owner could expect to exercise control. Almost all residences would face directly onto a public street, with a public street address, and the number of housing units would increase by almost 50 per cent. In the section of Edgeley studied intensively, the number of units would increase from 298 to 520, with most of the new units having front and back yards, with their own front door. Littlewood's plan calls for a return to the design of the older city, 'to create a sense of normality within the neighbourhood': units facing onto public roads, minimizing of common open space, and increasing the number of housing units to about twenty-five units per acre.

Architect A.J. Diamond provided a comparable redesign for the ten-acre Finch/Birchmount project in northeast Metro Toronto. This project was also designed in the 1960s and consists of 237 units in a twelve-storey slab apartment building and 120 townhouses on a private roadway system. The solutions proposed by the Diamond study parallel those suggested by Littlewood for Edgeley, including:

- Public roads through the site to give each townhouse a street address and a clearly defined public front and private back side to the house.
- New roads to allow through traffic on the site.
- Townhouses to relate squarely to the streetfront. Those townhouses that were built in a set-back pattern to create a zigzag facade should either be demolished or integrated into a square street pattern.
- Pedestrian paths through the site to be eliminated and all pedestrian traffic limited to street sidewalks.
- The park area to be clearly defined, with good surveillance from housing built on all four sides facing the park. Other open-space areas to be reduced to a minimum, with emphasis on providing more private outdoor space.
- Backyards to be private, and accessed only from the adjacent townhouse.
(Sewell 1988, 136–8)

The plan also proposes major changes to the way the interior of the apartment building works. The slab tower would be divided vertically into two independent sections, so each floor would have either nine or eleven units gaining access from it, rather than twenty-two at present. Internal corridors would be eliminated on the bottom two floors so that units – as well as the new commercial uses introduced such as a corner store, drycleaner, and management office – would have direct access from the outside. Fire stair exits would be located near main entrances to ensure better control, much as proposed by Newman for New York City apartment buildings. These changes

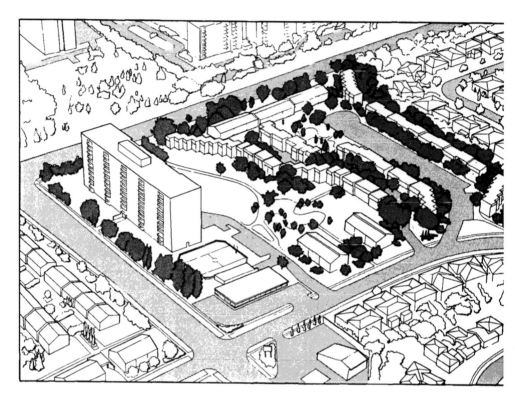

Existing Site Perspective

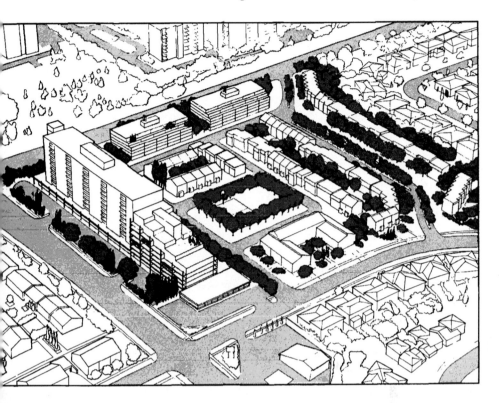

posed Site Perspective

Finch/Birchmount plan. The redesign by A.J. Diamond in 1987 proposes a series of public roads, including one that permits local access to Finch Avenue, thus ensuring through traffic. As well, housing has been regularized along public streets, which would have a sense of order and definition.
A.J. Diamond

would greatly reduce the uncontrolled quality of corridors and stairways inside the building.

The scheme substantially increases the number of housing units, from 357 to 578. Many of the new units are in six-storey apartment buildings, with a few dozen new units in a townhouse form. Fully developed, residential densities would be approximately fifty units per acre – five or six times that found in the surrounding low-density neighbourhood, but about half those in the St Lawrence community.

The preliminary reaction of local politicians to each scheme was instructive. Their general position was one of anger about the constant problems and complaints the projects seemed to generate. Redesign offered them the possibility of a good way to stem neighbourhood problems. The political concern was not with the proposed street system, increased density, or loss of open space: it was a fear that the new housing would be only for low-income tenants. If the politicians could be guaranteed that most of the new housing would be available as market housing rather than government-sponsored low-income housing, they indicated they would be supportive of the redesign. Unfortunately, provincial officials showed reluctance with proceeding, and neither project has been pursued.

The one redesign that gained the support of public housing authorities was that proposed for Moss Park, an urban renewal scheme discussed in chapter 5. The 1987 redesign proposed by Paul Reuber is simple: Seaton Street, which was closed when the project was built in 1962, would be reintroduced, and street-related townhouses and residential buildings would be built on an underused parking lot. This proposal was followed by other schemes calling for more substantial change, and, in 1992, they remain under discussion.

In *Building Cities That Work*, Fowler deals extensively with the growing body of literature analysing the social consequences of the corporate suburb, and, like Newman and Coleman, he concludes that 'the kind of urban environment we have built since World War II has significant social costs' (Fowler 1992, 98). He comes to the same conclusion about economic costs. After looking exhaustively at the direct and indirect costs of public

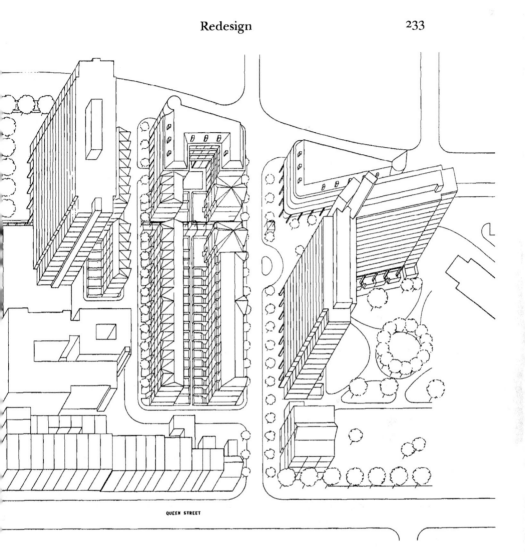

QUEEN STREET

Moss Park redesign. Paul Rueber, 1987. This plan calls for restoring Seaton
Street, which was closed for the scheme in the early 1960s, and building west
of the street. Paul Rueber

and private transportation (the former was touched on in chapter 7), he states: 'the pattern of deconcentrated and seg-regated land use is unacceptably expensive' (49). He reaches the same conclusion about other municipal services and about housing: 'The denser the settlement, the cheaper it is to provide sewers and to provide water' (50).

The evidence seems overwhelming that increasing suburban densities will reduce per capita servicing costs. The simplest way to increasing densities in existing suburban communities is to permit houses to be converted to two units, which has the possibility of almost doubling the residential density. This is a traditional city approach practised throughout North America in the nineteenth and twentieth centuries and it has many positive benefits. It provides added income to the homeowner to help meet mortgage costs, thus making homeownership more affordable. It provides each community with more resi-dents, creating more potential customers for nearby corner stores that otherwise do not have a large enough client base to be financially viable. More residents in the neighbourhood hold the promise of supporting good transit service, since there are more potential riders for existing routes. And this change can be accomplished with minimal physical disruption.

These arguments have, to date, not been convincing to any Toronto area municipalities where most of the housing has been built since mid-century. Instead, those municipalities prohibit this kind of individual choice, imposing zoning re-strictions that require all houses to be occupied only by one family – a natural follow-through to the separation of uses advocated in Don Mills, which restricted one kind of use to one kind of street. It should be noted that these zoning re-strictions are not universally admired: Scarborough officials have concluded that about 10 per cent of owners now rent out a second unit illegally, and a public opinion poll in 1989 con-cluded that about two-thirds of Scarborough residents had no real objection to second units. Yet suburban politicians have held tough, arguing that second units will cause parking prob-lems, perhaps sewage problems, and certainly building inspec-tion problems. The NIMBY syndrome – Not In My Backyard – is

widespread enough for politicians not to permit people to
make the small changes needed to introduce second units.

Suburban residents have bought the dream of security Taylor
offered in Don Mills: you will know the income of families on
your street are the same as yours because the housing and
financing costs are the same. Buying into Don Mills meant one
could buy into a world just like your own. This has been one of
the strongest attractions of the new suburbs, and permitting
tenants to live on any street would wreak havoc with notions of
suburban exclusivity.

As sketches prepared by A.J. Diamond in 1981 indicate,
suburban homes and the suburban streetscape undergo little
external change if conversion is done in a sensitive manner.
This is the simplest of redesigns, costing no public funds while
creating many housing opportunities. It only seems a matter
of time before some suburban council decides to make it a
possibility.

Not only have alternatives to existing projects and structures
been proposed, but viable alternatives to traditional greenfield
suburban development have been proposed by the development
industry itself. One proposal by the River Oaks Group in
Oakville, just to the west of Toronto, begins:

In both theory and application, an international trend is emerging
for community proposals fundamentally different from current
suburban development patterns. These proposals respond to a
range of concerns, from environmental to financial. They also
appear to be rooted in an intuitive recognition of the potential
richness of urban life offered by more compact and varied forms of
development, and the realization that the 'suburban dream' has
serious limitations.

These realizations, reflected in market surveys and municipal
politics, stem from the experienced shortcomings of existing low-
density, single-use development patterns. Suburbs can be socially
isolating ... Even the suburban advantage of offering proximity to
nature has virtually disappeared, as all traces of the natural environment are removed in the course of the development process ... New
thinking for the suburbs must reflect a re-evaluation of quality of

DON MILLS   *existing (1981)*

Don Mills house conversions, as proposed by A.J. Diamond, 1981. The figure on the left, a drawing of one corner of Don Mills, contains twenty-five units; the adaption on the right, forty units. Apart from the new structure replacing two houses at the right of the adaption drawing, new units are incorporated into existing houses or small additions. A.J. Diamond

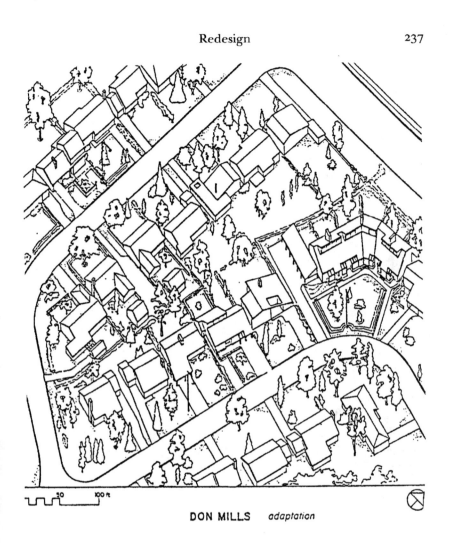

DON MILLS *adaptation*

life, and make further efforts to respect, and begin to repair, the natural environment. (Berridge 1991, 1)

The development company retained planners Berridge, Lewinberg, Greenberg to propose a plan for the sixteen-acre Sixth Line site part of the company's extensive holdings. The scheme proposed is based on a compact grid of streets and blocks; clearly defined public realm; compatibility with the natural environment (with particular attention to storm water retention and landscaping); and social diversity and affordability. A traditional suburban development for 225 units would occupy fifty acres: in this scheme, 225 units in house-form structures occupy sixteen acres.

The scheme has received preliminary approval from staff and politicians in Oakville, even though it breaks many traditional standards relating to lot size, unit mix, storm-water management, and road right-of-way widths. The report concludes:

Implementation of innovative plans like that proposed for Sixth Line will require a fresh look at development standards at all levels in order to promote rather than inhibit the development patterns described above. The overriding objective for new suburban communities like Sixth Line should be to broaden and diversify rather than restrict and homogenize. The focus of development and infrastructure standards must shift to acknowledge a whole new array of community goals including affordability, sociability, diversity, and environmental fit. (Berridge, Lewisberg, Greenberg 1991, 10)

A second large development company, the Daniels Group (headed by Jack Daniels, who was on the design team of Erin Mills), has provided its own manifesto for new design, and intends to proceed with a new community it calls 'Healthy Village.' The seventy-five-acre site is in Springdale, a 4000 acre community in Brampton. Springdale has been planned during the last decade in the Erin Mills manner, and construction began in 1991. As the Daniel manifesto notes:

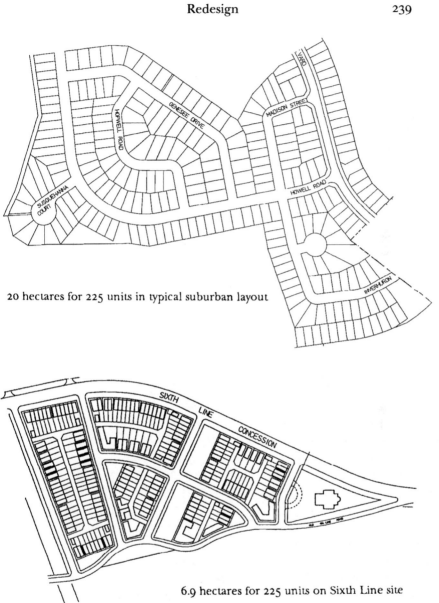

20 hectares for 225 units in typical suburban layout

6.9 hectares for 225 units on Sixth Line site

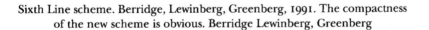

Sixth Line scheme. Berridge, Lewinberg, Greenberg, 1991. The compactness
of the new scheme is obvious. Berridge Lewinberg, Greenberg

Underlying our motivation in developing the Healthy Village model is our belief that conventional suburban land use planning is no longer valid. The dream of escaping the city for home ownership and a better lifestyle in the suburbs is becoming a social, economic and environmental nightmare.

It is no longer appropriate to turn our best agricultural land into sprawling low density suburbs. Reliance on the automobile, for both the five minute trip to the local strip plaza, as well as the hours of commuting to employment centres, cannot be sustained.

For the most part, however, land developers and the municipalities in which they work have yet to realize the need for change. Their combined efforts remain focused on building endless subdivisions of two storey detached 'garage-dominated' homes at six to eight units/acre. And for the most part, the developer's years of effort and financial risk are rewarded in the marketplace. The successful launch of the first phase of the new Springdale community has certainly reinforced the notion that the developer and the municipality are giving people what they want.

But what about the long term?
(Daniels 1991, 1-2)

The company proposes to develop a plan that has mixed land uses (including one job for every four residents), meaningful public spaces, housing intensification and a wide choice of dwelling types and tenures, and planning with the environment in mind, including district heating, electrical co-generation, and comprehensive recycling. The form that will contain these concepts has yet to be devised, although the company is proceeding to establish the vehicles for both planning and implementation. 'The Healthy Village,' the company notes, 'will be the opposite of the current three pole suburban models: low density single detached dwellings; high density high rise apartments; and shopping malls' (Daniels 1991, appendix, 3).

Sixth Line and Healthy Village may not become realities, but they do signal a change that is growing within the development industry itself – to rethink the basic elements of modern planning in Toronto suburbs. Lowell's line, as cited in the introduction to the first edition of Ebenezer Howard's book comes to mind: 'New occasions teach new duties.'

Bibliography

Adamson, A.A., and Eugene, Faludi. 1944. 'Toronto and Its Master Plan 1943.' Royal Architectural Institute of Canada, *Journal* 21, 6 (June): 111–34

Adamson, A.A. 1962. 'Form and the 20th Century Canadian City.' *Queen's Quarterly* 69 (spring): 49–68

Agnew, John, John Mercer, and David Sopha, eds. 1984. *The City in the Cultural Context*. London: Allen and Unwin

Allen, Irving Lewis, ed. 1977. *New Towns and the Suburban Dream*. Port Washington, NY: Kennikat Press

Architectural Forum (New York), June 1954, 148

Arthur, Eric. 1962. *No Mean City*. Toronto: University of Toronto Press

Artibise, Alan F.J., and Gilbert A. Stetler, eds. 1977. *The Canadian City*. Toronto: McClelland and Stewart

– 1986. *Power and Place: Canadian Urban Development in the North American Context*. Vancouver: University of British Columbia Press

Atwood, Margaret, ed. 1982. *The New Oxford Book of Canadian Verse*. Toronto: Oxford University Press

– 1970. *Journals of Susanna Moodie*. Toronto: Oxford University Press

Bacon, Edmund. 1974. *Design of Cities*. Revised edition. London: Penguin Books

Baird, George. 1974. *On Building Downtown*. Toronto: City of Toronto Planning Department

Baldassare, Mark. 1986. *Trouble in Paradise: The Suburban Transformation in America*. New York: Columbia University Press

Barker, Kent. 1951. 'Ajax: Planning a New Town in Ontario,' *Community Planning Review* 1 (February): 6

Bebout, Richard, ed. 1972. *The Open Gate: Toronto Union Station*. Toronto: Peter Martin Associates

Benevolo, Leonardo. 1967. *The Origins of Modern Town Planning*. London: Routledge & Kegan Paul

Berridge, Lewinberg, Greenberg, Ltd. 1991. *Revisiting the Suburbs: A Plan for the Sixth Line Community, River Oaks, Oakville*. Toronto

Bourne, Larry S., ed. 1971. *Internal Structure of the City*. Toronto: Oxford
     University Press
Bramalea Consolidated Development Limited. 1958. *Bramalea: Canada's First
     Satellite City*. Toronto
Buder, Stanley. 1990. *Visionaries and Planners*. New York: Oxford University
     Press
Bureau of Architecture and Urbanism. 1987. *Toronto Modern Architecture,
     1945–1965*. Toronto: Coach House Press
Bureau of Municipal Research. 1972. 'Toronto Region's Privately Developed
     New Communities.' *Civic Affairs*, no. 2, 6–20
Burke, Gill, ed. 1980. *Housing and Social Justice*. London: Longman
Callaghan, Morley. 1966. *More Joy in Heaven*. Toronto: McClelland and Stewart
Careless, J.M.S. 1984. *Toronto to 1918: An Illustrated History*. Toronto: James
     Lorimer
Carver, Humphrey. 1946. 'Reconstruction News.' Toronto Reconstruction
     Council, 15 Feb.
– 1948. *Houses for Canadians*. Toronto: University of Toronto Press
– 1962. *Cities in the Suburbs*. Toronto: University of Toronto Press
– 1975. *Compassionate Landscape*. Toronto: University of Toronto Press
Caulfield, John. 1974. *Tiny Perfect Mayor*. Toronto: James Lorimer
Central Ontario Lakeshore Urban Complex (COLUC). 1974. *Report to the
     Adivisory Committee on Urban and Regional Planning*. December
Christensen, Carol A.1986. *The American Garden City and the New Towns
     Movement*. Ann Arbor: UMI Research Press
CityHome Report. 1979. Toronto: City of Toronto Non-Profit Housing
     Corporation
City of Toronto Planning Department. 1955. 'Regent Park South Redevelop-
     ment Study'
– 1985. 'St. Jamestown Revitalization'
Clark, S.D. 1966. *The Suburban Society*. Toronto: University of Toronto Press
Clay, Charles. 1958. *The Leaside Story*. Leaside, Ont.: Leaside Council
Coleman, Alice. 1985. *Utopia on Trial: Vision and Reality in Planned Housing*.
     London: Hilary Shipman
Comay Planning Consultants Ltd. 1973. *Subject to Approval*. Toronto: Ontario
     Economic Council
Committee to Enquire into Housing Conditions in Several Areas of the City
     of Toronto. 1934. *Report of the Lieutenant-Governor's Committee on Housing
     Conditions in Toronto, 1934* [Bruce Report]. Toronto: Hunter-Rose
Community Development Consultants Ltd. [1971]. *Malvern: Development
     Plan & Programme*. Toronto: A Joint Project of the Federal and Provincial
     Governments

Core Area Task Force. 1974. *Summary and Recommendations.* City of Toronto
Planning Board

Cullingworth, Barry. 1984. 'The Provincial Role in Planning and Development.' *Plan Canada* 24(3 and 4):142

Daniels Group. 1991. *Healthy Village Planning Model.* Toronto

Danielson, Michael. 1976. *The Politics of Exclusion.* New York: Columbia
University Press

Davies, Robertson. 1972. *The Manticore.* New York: Viking

Dendy, William. 1978. *Lost Toronto.* Toronto: Oxford University Press

Dendy, William, and William Kilbourn, 1986. *Toronto Observed.* Toronto:
Oxford University Press

Design Quarterly (Minneapolis), issue 108, 1978

Diamond, A.J., Planners Ltd. 1981. *Increasing Suburban Densities.* Toronto

Dolce, Philip C., ed. 1976. *Suburbia.* Garden City, NY: Anchor Press/
Doubleday

Don Mills Development Corp. 1969. *Erin Mills.* Toronto

Edwards, Arthur M. 1981. *The Design of Suburbia.* London: Pembridge Press

Erin Mills Newsletter. 1981. Mississauga: Don Mills Development Corporation.
Spring

Erin Mills, New Town. 1969. Toronto: Don Mills Development Corporation

Ernst and Hickerson, eds. 1985 *Urban America: Documenting the Planners.*
Catalogue for exhibition at Cornell University, October

Environments. 1985. Waterloo: University of Waterloo

Faludi, Eugene. 1944. Papers. Metro Toronto Reference Library, Toronto.

– 1946. 'Plans for Eight Communities.' Royal Architectural Institute of
Canada, *Journal* 23, 11: 276–93

– 1947. *A Master Plan for the Development of the City of Hamilton.* City Panning
Committee of Hamilton

– 1950. 'Designing New Canadian Communities.' American Institute of
Planners, *Journal* 16 (2): 71–9; (3): 147

– ed. 1952. *Land Development in the Metropolitan Area of Toronto.* Toronto:
Toronto Real Estate Board

Fishman, Robert. 1977. *Urban Utopias in the 20th Century.* New York: Basic
Books

– 1987. *Bourgeois Utopias.* New York: Basic Books

Fowler, Edmund P. 1992. *Building Cities That Work.* Montreal: McGill-
Queen's University Press

Fox, Howard, and Michael Winton. 1979. 'St Jamestown.' Unpublished
manuscript

Fraser, Graham. 1972. *Fighting Back: Urban Renewal in Trefann Court.*
Toronto: Hakkert

Fraser, Graham, Jay Richardson, David Wood, and Dennis Wood. 1974. *Tail of the Elephant.* Toronto: Pollution Probe

Freedman, Adele. 1990. *Sight Lines.* Toronto: Oxford University Press

Gertler, L.O., ed. 1968. *Planning the Canadian Environment.* Montreal: Harvest House

Gibson, J.E. 1977. *Designing the New City.* New York: John Wiley and Sons

Girouard, Mark. 1985. *Cities and People.* New Haven: Yale University Press

Goodman, Percival and Paul. 1947. *Communitas.* Chicago: University of Chicago Press

Gosling, David, and Barry Maitland. 1984. *Concepts of Urban Design.* New York: Academy Editions/St Martin's Press

Hall, Peter. 1988. *Cities of Tomorrow.* Oxford: Basil Blackwell

Hancock, Macklin, and Douglas H. Lee. 1954. Royal Architechural Institute of Canada, *Journal* 31 (1): 3

Hayden, Dolores. 1981. *The Grand Domestic Revolution: A History of Feminist Designs for American Homes, Neighbourhoods, and Cities.* Cambridge, Mass.: Massachusetts Institute of Technology

Hellyer, Paul. 1969. *Federal Task Force on Housing and Urban Development.* Ottawa: Queen's Printer

Hitchcock, John R., and Anne McMaster, eds. 1985. *The Metropolis: Proceedings of a Conference in Honour of Hans Blumenfeld.* Toronto: Governing Council, University of Toronto

Hodge, Gerald. 1986. *Planning Canadian Communities.* Toronto: Methuen

Hohenberg, Paul M., and Lynn Hollen Lees. 1985. *The Making of Urban Europe, 1000–1950.* Cambridge, Mass.: Harvard University Press

Hohl, R. 1968. *Office Buildings, an International Survey.* New York: Praeger

Hornbeck, James. 1961. 'The New Skyscraper.' In *Architectural Record: Office Buildings.* New York: F.W. Dodge

Hough, Michael. 1984. *City Form and Natural Process.* New York: Van Nostrand Reinhold

Housing Authority of Toronto. 1951. *Regent Park (North) Housing Project.* Toronto: City Hall

Housing Department, City of Toronto. 1974–6. *St Lawrence Project Studies*

Howard, Ebenezer. 1965. *Garden Cities of Tomorrow.* Cambridge, Mass.: Massachusetts Institute of Technology

Hulchanski, J.D. 1978. 'Thomas Adams and Lindenlea.' Unpublished manuscript

Jackson, Kenneth T. 1985. *Crabgrass Frontier.* New York: Oxford University Press

Jacobs, Jane. 1961. *The Death and Life of Great American Cities.* New York: Vintage Books

- 1984. *Cities and the Wealth of Nations.* New York: Random House
Johnson-Marshall, Percy. 1966. *Rebuilding Cities.* Chicago: Aldine Publishing
Lasker, David. 'The Split Level Dream'. 1985. *Ontario Living,* October
Leacock, Stephen. 1947. *Sunshine Sketches of a Little Town.* Toronto:
McClelland and Stewart
Lees, Andrew. 1985. *Cities Perceived: Urban Society in European and American Thought, 1820–1940.* Manchester: Manchester University Press
Lemon, James. 1985. *Toronto since 1918.* Toronto: James Lorimer
Lorimer, James. 1970. *The Real World of City Politics.* Toronto: James Lewis and Samuel
- 1971. *Working People.* Toronto: James Lewis and Samuel
- 1978. *The Developers.* Toronto: James Lorimer
Lorimer, James, and Evelyn Ross, eds. 1977. *The Second City Book.* Toronto: James Lorimer
Lynch, Kevin. 1981. *Good City Form.* Cambridge, Mass.: Massachusetts Institute of Technology
McConnell, Shean. 1959. 'The Neighbourhood,' *Canadian Planning Review* 9, 3 (Sept.): 82
MacInnis, Grace. 1953. *J.S. Woodsworth, a Man to Remember.* Toronto: Macmillan
McKeough, Darcy. 1974. *Status Report on the Toronto-Centred Region.* Ministry of Treasury, Economics, and Intergovernmental Affairs, Province of Ontario. August
MacLennan, High. 1945. *Two Solitutes.* Toronto: Popular Library
- 1959. *The Watch That Ends the Night.* Toronto: New American Library
Markusen, J.R., and D.T. Scheffman. 1977. *Speculation and Monopoly in Urban Development.* Toronto: Economic Council of Ontario
Mathers, A.S. 1940. 'Housing and Building Construction.' Royal Architectural Institute of Canada, *Journal* 17(5): 69–74
Metropolitan Toronto and Region Transportation Study. 1967. *Choices for a Growing Region.* Toronto: Department of Municipal Affairs, Community Planning Branch
Metropolitan Toronto Planning Board. 1962. 'District 10 Plan.' February
Metropolitan Toronto Planning Department. 1980. *Metroplan*
Ministry of Agriculture and Food, 1978. *Food Land Guidelines.* Toronto: Government of Ontario
Ministry of Housing. 1976. *Urban Development Standards.* Toronto
Morton, Desmond. 1973. *Mayor Howland.* Toronto: Hakkert
Mumford, Lewis. 1961. *The City in History.* New York: Harcourt Brace Jovanovich
Newman, Oscar. 1973. *Defensible Space.* New York: Macmillan

- 1981. *Community of Interest.* Garden City, NY: Anchor Books/Doubleday
Nowlan, David and Nadine. 1970. *The Bad Trip: The Untold Story of the Spadina Expressway.* Toronto: New Press/House of Anansi
Oberlander, Peter and Cornelia. 1956. 'Critique: Canada's New Towns.' *Progressive Architecture,* 9: 113–9
Pendergrast, Eudora. 1981. *Suburbanizing the Central City.* Papers on Planning and Design, Deptartment of Urban and Regional Planning, University of Toronto
Perry, Clarence. 1939. *Housing for the Machine Age.* New York: Russell Sage Foundation
Phillips, Nathan. 1967. *Mayor of All the People.* Toronto: McClelland and Stewart
Pickett, Stanley. 1957. 'Planning and Urban Renewal.' *Community Planning Review* 7 (3): 129
Planning and Development Department, City of Toronto. 1984. 'Dreams of Development'
Powell, Alan, ed. 1972. *The City: Attacking Modern Myths.* Toronto: McClelland and Stewart
Pressman, Norman E.P. 1976. *New Communities in Canada.* Waterloo: Faculty of Environmental Studies, University of Waterloo
Relph, Edward. 1987. *The Modern Urban Landscape.* Baltimore: Johns Hopkins University Press
Rennick, Kathleen. 1986. 'The Town of Leaside, Origins and Development, 1913–39.' Toronto. Unpublished manuscript
Richards, J.M. 1948. *An Introduction to Modern Architecture.* Harmondsworth: Pelican
Richardson, Nigel. 1981. 'Insubstantial Pageant: The Rise and Fall of Provincial Planning in Ontario.' *Canadian Public Administration,* 24, 4, (winter): 563–86
- ed. 1984. 'Special Issue on Golden Age of Planning in Ontario, 1965–1975.' *Plan Canada* 24, 3/4, December
Rohmer, Richard. 1978. *E.P. Taylor.* Toronto: McClelland and Stewart
Rose, Albert. 1958. *Regent Park.* Toronto: University of Toronto Press
- 1972. *Governing Metropolitan Toronto: A Social and Political Analysis, 1953–1971.* Berkeley: University of California Press
Russell, Victor, ed. 1984. *Forging a Consensus: Historical Essays on Toronto.* Toronto: University of Toronto Press
Rutherford, Paul, ed. 1974. *Saving the Canadian City: The First Phase, 1880–1920.* Toronto: University of Toronto Press
Schaffer, Daniel. 1982. *Garden Cities for America: The Radburn Experience.* Philadelphia: Temple University Press

Sewell, John. 1972. *Up Against City Hall.* Toronto: James Lorimer
– 1988. 'Key MTHA Documents,' an appendix to 'Changing MTHA.' Toronto: Metro Toronto Housing Authority. November
– 1992. 'Suburbs Then and Now.' Unpublished
Soberman, Richard M. 1975. *Choices for the Future.* Toronto: Metropolitan Toronto Plan Review
Spelt, Jacob. 1973. *Toronto.* Toronto: Collier Macmillan
Spurr, Peter. 1976. *Land and Urban Development.* Toronto: James Lorimer
Stein, Clarence. 1951. *Toward New Towns for America.* Liverpool: University Press of Liverpool
Stern, Robert A.M. 1981. *The Anglo-American Suburb.* Architectural Design Profile. London: St Martin's Press
Sutton, S.B., ed. 1971. *Civilizing American Cities: A Selection of Frederick Law Olmstead's Writings.* Cambridge, Mass.: MIT Press
Tafuri, Manfredo. 1976. *Architecture and Utopia.* Cambridge, Mass.: Massachusetts Institute of Technology
Thompson, F.M.L. 1982. *The Rise of Suburbia.* Leicester: Leicester University Press
Toronto and York Planning Board. 1949. 'Report No. 1.' December
Treasury, Economics and Intergovernmental Affairs Department. 1984. *Central Ontario Lakeshore Urban Complex.* Province of Ontario
University Planners, Architects and Consulting Engineers (UPACE). 1962. *Master Plan, York University.* Toronto
Unwin, Sir Raymond. 1918. *Nothing Gained by Overcrowding.* London: Garden Cities and Town Planning Association
Van Nostrand, John. 'Toronto's Suburbs: Their Origins and Future.' Unpublished manuscript
Von Moos, Stanislaw. 1979. *Le Corbusier, Elements of a Synthesis.* Cambridge, Mass.: MIT Press
White, Morton and Lucia. 1977. *The Intellectual versus the City.* Oxford: Oxford University Press. First printed 1962
Wright, Frank Lloyd. 1958. *The Living City.* New York: Horizon Press

The author wishes to thank those who gave permission for the use of illustrations and other material. Thanks also to University College, University of Toronto, for the 1988 invitation to give four lectures on urban planning – lectures that proved the impetus for this book.

Index